Only A Few

Is Jesus Your First Love?

Book 2

Daniel J.
[God is my Judge]

ONLY A FEW – Book 2

Copyright

© 2020 All rights reserved. No part of this book may be reproduced without the written permission of the author at daniel.j7x7@gmail.com

ISBN: 9798574435601
Imprint: Independently published

Bible References
Unless indicated otherwise, all Scripture quotations are taken from The Holy Bible, New International Version® NIV® Copyright © 1973 1978 1984 2011 by Biblica, Inc. TM Used by permission. All rights reserved worldwide.

Scriptures marked as "(GNT)" are taken from the Good News Translation - Second Edition © 1992 by American Bible Society. Used by permission.

Scripture quotations are taken from the Holy Bible, New Living Translation (marked 'NLT'), copyright ©1996, 2004, 2007, 2013, 2015 by Tyndale House Foundation. Used by permission of Tyndale House Publishers, Inc., Carol Stream, Illinois 60188. All rights reserved.

Scripture quotations marked "NKJV" are taken from the New King James Version. Copyright © 1982 by Thomas Nelson, Inc. Used by permission. Used by permission of Thomas Nelson, Inc. All rights reserved.

When emphases were added to quoted Scripture texts, this author has omitted the customary '(emphasis added)' qualification so as not to interrupt the flow of the book. Any and all visible emphases must be considered added by the author, whether underlined, italicised, emboldened and/or upper case.

Out of reverence for God, the author has also capitalised all pronoun references to the Person of God, the Father, Jesus and the Holy Spirit where they do not appear in the original texts.

With Grateful Thanks

Firstly, my deepest gratitude to my Father for calling me and drawing me near when I deserve the opposite. To my Lord and Master, Jesus Christ, for His incredible gift. To the Spirit for leading me on this journey and in writing this book. To the Lord God, I am forever thankful for Your great mercies and grace!

To my family: my wife who faithfully walked this journey with me. Now we look forward to the next phase of this journey together as our Loving God leads us. To my children, whether natural or adopted by marriage to one of ours: you have seen first-hand my journey. May it serve as a humble example of God's mercies when we intentionally follow Jesus as our First Love, even when every earthly evidence is against following His words. To my grandchildren: may it serve as an inspiration for the years to come when life may become very confusing, yet there is one place where you will find a Solid Rock for your feet: Jesus Himself. To my brother who spent many hours trawling through the text, your support was invaluable!

'Now to Him who is able to do so much more than all we ask or imagine, according to His power that is at work within us, to Him be the glory in the church and in Christ Jesus throughout all generations, forever and ever. Amen' (***Ephesians 3:20-21***).

Contents

1 Foreword 1
2 Summary of Book 1 4
3 Pathway to the Gate 14
4 Mind Before Heart 53
5 Seeking to Find Jesus 72
6 The 'Second Call' 106
7 Water Baptism 112
8 Enter in: Find Jesus, Receive the Spirit 136
9 Famous Christians 179
10 When God Waits 191
11 On the Narrow Road 196
12 A Major Divide, A Heart-Breaking Reality ... 215
13 Parting Comments 223

1 Foreword

When athletes set their sights on the Olympic Games it fully dominates their lives: from getting up in the morning to going to bed at night, their daily routine, their nutrition and their exercise regime. They give attention to every small detail that will increase their performance. They cut out ruthlessly anything that negatively affects their performance, even if they only suspect it may. It is their all-consuming passion, their single greatest pursuit and their total focus. They narrow their interests and most athletes fit other things, even their relationships, around their main pursuit.

They know if they allow other passions to take a greater priority they will not achieve their goal. Their routine and focus continue to the end. There is no holiday from preparing for the greatest pursuit of their lives.

How do they arrive at this point? They choose what they want to achieve, they dedicate their lives to it, they make every effort and they continue until they achieve.

Many people have dreams of becoming Olympic athletes, yet the majority don't go through with it once they realise what is involved. It is easy to say 'yes', but to continue once the cost is clear is a different matter. It's not their early decision that counts, but whether they push through until they succeed. Many cannot wave goodbye to competing loves and cut out distractions - the goal just isn't important enough to sacrifice it all. This one pursuit must stand above all else or success will not come. Shared passions or a second priority will not do.

This is also the true Christian life, just vastly more. It is a life surrendered and a mind fixated on Jesus, but for life. Medals are temporary and for personal glory; following Christ is for all of this life, for all of eternity and for God's glory.

God loves the world to the extent that He sent His own Son to die for our sins so that we need not be punished. Yet His love goes further: He also wants to give us a life of true joy and peace in Jesus on the earth, and to be one with Him eternally.

We gain access to God and His love by loving Him back and by truly believing in His Son.

Jesus must be 'head and shoulders' above all competing loves: '*If anyone comes to Me and does not hate father and mother, wife and children, brothers and sisters – yes, even their own life – such a person cannot be My disciple*' (**_Luke 14:26_**). The translation of the original Greek word into 'hate' is not very helpful in this setting. How can Jesus expect us to hate our relatives?! Everyone has been confused by this statement at some stage. But the word also means to renounce one choice in favour of another and a moral choice that elevates one option over another. This is clearer, yet there is an essence of the 'hate' translation that must be retained – a harshness of choice. In reality Jesus was saying that when I list the loves in my life, He cannot just be one of them, or be slotted in at the top my list of loves, forcing all others a little lower. He insists on being right at the top of the page, in positions 1 - 30, and my other loves only start after that. This is to 'hate' my life and other loves compared to Jesus.

This kind of choice doesn't happen by itself. It requires a clear decision and resolute commitment. I must choose Him, even take pre-decisions, so that I already know the answer when competing loves come knocking. If we want Jesus, we must trim our appetites, stake out our boundaries, declare our intentions and untie ourselves from all that binds us. This is the first-choice love of the true follower: to love the Lord my God with all my heart, soul, mind and strength.

An aspiring Olympic athlete decides to go flat-out for their goal for the love of the sport, fame, financial benefit, etc. For the true follower their motivation is to find and remain with Jesus! That alone is the highest purpose.

Let us come to this book in the full knowledge of God's love and with the understanding that we can only find Jesus in God's way. Jesus must be my clear first choice, not an added extra. This book is dedicated to finding Jesus in God's way.

Before you start, please ask God to guide you by His Spirit.

2 Summary of Book 1

This book follows on from Book 1 under the same title. We will start with a brief summary of the first book. If you haven't read Book 1 yet, I really recommend that you do that first. Many of our discussions will assume a working understanding of what we already covered.

'Only a Few'

In **Matthew 7:21-23** Jesus foretells a real situation that <u>will</u> happen at the Judgement: *"Not everyone who says to Me, 'Lord, Lord,' will enter the kingdom of heaven, but only the one who does the will of My Father who is in heaven. Many will say to Me on that day, 'Lord, Lord', did we not prophesy in Your name and in Your name drive out demons and in Your name perform many miracles?' Then I will tell them plainly, 'I never knew you. Away from Me, you evildoers!'"*

Jesus also spoke of a similar situation in **Luke 13:24-27** *'... many, I tell you, will try to enter and will not be able to. Once the owner of the house gets up and closes the door, you will stand outside knocking and pleading, "Sir, open the door for us." But he will answer, "I don't know you or where you come from. Then you will say, "We ate and drank with You, and You taught in our streets." But he will reply, "I don't know you or where you come from. Away from Me, all you evildoers!"* There will be many who will come, expecting to be let in due to their presence in church, their extensive spiritual acts and their work for God. They believe these are proof of their right relationship with Him. And yet, Jesus will say He <u>never</u> knew them.

It isn't necessary to study the original Greek texts to get a clear grasp of what Jesus said and meant. His words are clear enough from all modern translations. When we read <u>all His words</u> in the Gospels we are left in no uncertainty as to what He wants us to know. I only add a small number of original text references to help drive the points home quicker, yet no-one can claim that Jesus' intentions are not clear unless we study the original texts and that the true meaning is therefore hidden from Christians. That is simply not true.

The original Greek translated into 'knew' (*'I never knew you'*) speaks of much more than having met someone or even being well-acquainted. Instead it means having a deep, first-hand and personal experience and knowledge of the other person. The word is also used for an intimate relationship within marriage, such as in **<u>Luke 1:34</u>** when Mary questioned the angel Gabriel about her pregnancy: *'How can this be, since I do not <u>know</u> a man?'* (NKJV), or translated differently *'since I am a virgin'* (NIV). When we link this understanding with Jesus' words in **<u>Matthew 10:37</u>** *'Anyone who loves their father or mother more than Me is not worthy of Me; anyone who loves their son or daughter more than Me is not worthy of Me'*, then Jesus clearly intended a deep loving relationship. (This verse alone makes Greek references unnecessary!)

These teachings of Jesus hang together with **<u>Matthew 7:13-14</u>** *'Enter through the narrow gate. For wide is the gate and broad is the road that leads to destruction, and many enter through it. But small is the gate and narrow the road that leads to life, and only a few find it'*, and **<u>Luke 13:24</u>** *'Make every effort to enter through the narrow door, because many, I tell you, will try to enter and will not be able to'*. It is obvious from a plain reading of Jesus' words that salvation is not just a question of believing that He died for our sins and the basic facts about Jesus on the earth and that He will return.

Nor is it making a sincere commitment or even of being extensively used in God's work in the church. Yes, every engagement and marriage starts with a sincere commitment, but it must go further. Similarly Jesus demands something deeper, and He is not saying 'try harder' or 'do more'.

The original Greek word translated into 'only a few' ('*only a few find it*') is '*oligos*', which means a small or negligible proportion. And the word translated into 'many' is '*polis*', meaning multitudinous or a great majority. This isn't about the numerical percentages of salvation, - you can decide what these words mean to you. But Jesus is clear that a very large number of all those who call Him '*Lord, Lord*' will be sent to eternal damnation and that only a small proportion will find eternal life. Why? Because He judges the true heart. (For a full discussion on this point, please refer to Chapter 4 in Book 1.)

Jesus died for us. God calls us because He doesn't want any to go lost. He draws us, yet we must respond. God tells us what kind of response He wants from us and He only gives the Spirit rebirth when He sees a complete human heart change. This is a human level decision to love Jesus, acted out.

Message to the Church!

Jesus intended for us to sit up and take note of what He says.

The words of Jesus in Matthew 7:13-14 and 7:21-23 were recorded specifically for professing!

Read the **Matthew 7:21-23** again. How can those words be for anyone else? They are for the church, even 'choice members' in our churches: '*did we not prophesy in Your name and in Your name drive out demons and in Your name perform many miracles?*'

Jesus wants hard-working church people in ministries, who read their Bibles and pray, go on mission, lead churches and worship, to hear these words so they don't fall foul of His serious warnings! He didn't come to condemn the world, but to save the world (***John 12:47***). This isn't His angry message but His deep concern for all who call themselves Christian. It's a <u>loving advance warning</u> so that professing Christians will test themselves and <u>not</u> be called 'evildoers'.

Jesus stated a fact. It is up to us, under Spirit, to recognise if His warnings apply to us or not

---

The Small Gate and the Narrow Road

To find Jesus is available to everyone, but each one must come in His way. He is found only within the narrow boundaries that God declares, to the end of our lives. Entering by the narrow gate of Jesus is the point at which salvation is granted.

There is an unwritten agreement in Christianity that we are saved when we decide to follow Jesus, 'become a Christian' or pray a prayer, i.e. by our action. Yet this is not true; it is merely the start of the journey! It is God who opens the gate for us once He is satisfied that deep in our hearts we are really committed to Jesus. Salvation is not a contract, already signed by God, that only requires our signature to be activated. Instead, God sees us signing, then He assesses our hearts before He accepts us for the Bride of His precious Son.

This approval does not come from long years of service or earnest commitments, but in true repentance, faith and love for Jesus. God gives spiritual rebirth when He is satisfied with my heart, which shows in whether I do what He says (*'Whoever has My commands and keeps them is the one who* loves Me. The one who loves Me will be loved by My Father, and I too will love them and show Myself to them' **John 14:21**). God isn't looking for spiritual gold diggers who just want heaven or a good life on this earth. He wants those who really want Jesus because He gave His life for them.

Rebirth (entering by the small gate) is the point at which we receive the Holy Spirit (***v16-17*** *'And I will ask the Father, and He will give you another advocate to help you and be with you forever – the Spirit of truth'*), Jesus reveals Himself to us (***v21*** *'The one who loves Me will be loved by My Father, and I too will love them and show Myself to them'*) and God makes us one with Him (***v23*** *'My Father will love them, and We will come to them and make Our home with them'*). Yet, each of these passages is preceded by the same pattern: the one who loves Jesus is recognised by obedience, and the one who obeys is the one who truly loves Him. They are circular statements. Love for Jesus and obedience to His commands are directly linked – the one is the evidence of the other (this pattern is evident numerous times in Scripture). Note Jesus does not say obedience gives salvation, but that obedience shows love for Jesus! It's our abandon and obedience, not our words, prayers or service, that show we love Jesus and that we died to ourselves. This is the natural outworking of true faith.

God selects us for the Bride of His Son in His grace once we already showed our full surrender. Note that God is not looking for 100% obedience before He grants salvation, but a heart that is fully surrendered and therefore receptive to obey all that He says. ***1 John 2:4*** reads *'Whoever says, "I know Him," but does not do what He commands is a liar, and the truth is not in that person'*. If we continue to sin wilfully, we'll be well advised to read ***1 John 3:6*** *'No one who lives in Him keeps on sinning. No one who continues to sin has either seen Him or known Him'*. In practice this means that if you are addicted and then reborn by the Spirit, your addiction won't disappear overnight. It may, but usually not. Yet the Spirit stirs us and we won't stay in unbroken sin longer term. The Spirit helps us to overcome.

Saving Faith

The result of assuming salvation when we pray a sincere prayer is that we assume we obtain salvation by becoming the judge of our own faith. This is untenable.

---

*We cannot believe enough to get into heaven. Only the faith that Jesus authors, saves (**Heb 12:2**)*

Anything we do, including to believe, falls short of God's measure. We exercise our human level faith in Jesus and step out in obedience, but this faith does not save. God is not obliged to save me because I claim to believe. That is salvation by works, and makes a mockery of God's holiness. Instead, Paul says *'For it is by grace you have been saved, through faith — and this is not from yourselves, it is the gift of God — not by works, so that no one can boast'* (**Eph 2:8-9**). I believe and decide to follow but I am the same sinner worthy of hell. Yet God sees my surrendered heart and saves us by His grace.

When we are reborn by the Spirit, the memory of our rebirth and the ongoing testimony of the Spirit give us the hope and certainty described in **Hebrews 11:1** *'Now faith is confidence in what we hope for and assurance about what we do not see'*. This gives us irrefutable confidence that we have been saved. Only this faith which we get when we meet Jesus, saves. It does not come from ourselves. And it's evidence will show in obeying Jesus' commands out of gratitude and love.

In book 1 we also covered many typical proof-claims people make to substantiate their salvation, e.g. that God answers our prayers. However, this is not the evidence of salvation. The true internal evidence is the testimony of the Spirit, lived out in obedience externally. We will discuss the Spirit in greater detail later.

The Journey to Salvation

In Chapter 11 of Book 1 we mentioned different 'routes' to describe the pathway to salvation. We will use the 'Journey of the Heart' for our upcoming discussions as it avoids the pitfalls of un-Biblical shortcuts. The following are elements of this journey, but it certainly isn't a tick list of tasks to perform.

- 'Come and See' – Decide if you can Follow Me!
- The fear of the Lord is the beginning of all wisdom
- Being gifted Godly sorrow
- Repentance and a commitment to obey Jesus' teachings
- Whole-heartedly seek, ask and knock to find Jesus
- Learn about, believe in and trust in the divine Jesus
- Lose my own life (die to myself), surrender to Christ
- Deny myself, pick up my cross and follow Jesus
- Love Jesus as First Love
- A heart chosen by God and receiving the Spirit of Christ.

There is also a chapter on water baptism, which is not included in the elements above.

Our Faith and The Bible

The reason why church people call themselves Christian, attending services, serve, etc. is because of the words of the Bible, which we profess to be true. <u>Yet, if we are so sure we are saved by some verses of the Bible, why do we ignore or oppose</u>

other verses from the very same Book and the same speaker (Jesus)? This is illogical!

If we call ourselves Christian, should we not be serious about everything God says? If we gave the words of Jesus to unbelievers and asked what they thought we should do about them, they will definitely say we should obey them! In this argument you will find God on the side of the unbeliever! We say we believe in the Almighty God, believe the Bible is God's Word and that we follow Jesus who is God's Son, so the proof of our faith should be that we do what God says, shouldn't it?! Especially if the Word tells us to do so repeatedly.

How do we explain our odd (deadly) behaviour of ignoring so much of the Bible as if it isn't true?

It is time for us to make up our minds whether we are in or out, <u>following the Christ of the Bible or not</u>! This is core to the message of 'Only a Few'. If we don't take God's Word seriously, we will keep poking holes in the words from God we don't like – to our own eternal destruction!

The Disciple of Christ

The modern church movement has a deadly hate of doing what God commands and calls it 'salvation by works'. Yet Jesus said *'Therefore go and make disciples of all nations, baptising them in the name of the Father and of the Son and of the Holy Spirit, and teaching them to obey everything I have commanded you'* (**<u>Mat 20:19-20</u>**). His true disciples have a mindset to obey. And He goes further: He confirmed that His words came from the Father (**<u>John 12:49</u>**) and His words will be the basis of our judgement (*'There is a judge for the one who rejects Me and does not accept My words; the very* *words I have spoken will condemn them at the last day'* **John 12:48**). Could it be any clearer?

HELPS Word-Studies gives the meaning of the Greek word for disciple (*mathētés*) as *'a learner; a disciple, a follower of Christ who learns the doctrines of Scripture and the lifestyle they require; someone catechised* (instructed) *with proper instruction from the Bible with its necessary follow-through (life-applications)'.* True disciples follow Christ as Saviour and Lord, hear (study, listen, learn, seek out) what He says, and do it. It is a 'holy package'.

Some disciples follow loosely – the Many. Others follow closely – the Few. We must each choose how we will follow.

Let us keep this at the forefront of our minds as we study further.

Final Words Before We Start

This was a short overview of the essence of Book 1. We will now explore further what is true salvation according to the Word of God. Please keep in mind the following points that were made at the start of Book 1:

- Please look up all Bible references and read them in their context. This is a journey of discovering God's truth, not gullibly accepting what is in this book.

- There is an intentional level of repetition of some concepts and passages because we may need to reset our minds to the Truth of God. This may take several exposures. Please don't dismiss the repetition; rather ask if you have changed your mind and your life. We must take note because God's Word isn't wallpaper,! Christians read over God's warnings, truths, preconditions and commands all the time. If they don't change our entire being, then we have missed God Himself!

- The word 'the church' comes up regularly. Any discerning believer will realise we have a wide range of beliefs under the broad banner of Christianity. They cannot all be right. There is no 'broad church' with God, only His words and His ways are approved. Many beliefs of churches, leaders and professing believers are not Biblical. References to the church is not an assumption that all churches suffer from the same issues, but that wrong beliefs are widespread.

Lastly, don't rush through the book to put it on the shelf. Spend time with God. Ask Him to confirm His truth. Make it a matter between you and God, long before discussing it with others. It is far more important to open your spiritual ears intentionally to God than hear the views of someone. Take God and His Word seriously, regardless of the views of others. Rely on Him. He will teach you the truth (***Ps 32:8***).

You may be the only one in your religious family or gathering to decide to live by the truth of God. May you remain standing. I pray God will enlighten you by His Spirit.

3 Pathway to the Gate

The purpose of our discussions of '*Perspective 3: Journey of the Heart*' is three-fold:

- To help those who truly seek, to find Christ in God's way.
- To help them find quickly rather than spend years in deficient faith.
- To wake up those who think they are saved, but aren't.

It is reckless to teach the Gospel inaccurately – people may spend years in a spiritual desert, looking for the truth or never finding it. Worse still, they will spread the same inaccuracies further. '*If anyone speaks, they should do so as one who speaks the very words of God*' (**1 Pet 4:11**). Let us be diligent to teach only what is true and complete.

We will discuss words and commands of Jesus arranged broadly into a progressive sequence of faith steps. In practice many points overlap so distinctions may become somewhat blurred. The journey may also be on several fronts at the same time or be in a different 'sequence'. Rather than create 'stages' of faith the purpose of our discussions is to appreciate how radically our priorities change when we follow Jesus closely.

Hearing the Gospel

We start the pathway to the narrow gate of Jesus when we hear the Gospel, whether at an event, at home or anywhere else. Jesus said we cannot come to Him ourselves, but we must be drawn by the Father (***John 6:44***). Hearing the Gospel is one part of being drawn by the Father.

The Gospel is profound; it brings together life-defining truths in a single message and it makes great claims. It is counter-cultural and especially foreign to the modern mind that is hostile even to the idea of a Higher Power, let alone submitting to Him and being accountable to Him.

We may have been around church a long time and don't think of the scope of the Gospel anymore. Yet people are challenged with great claims – and so should we!

1. Of God – That God exists beyond any doubt. He is unseen, yet He is the Creator of everything that exists (not evolution or Big Bangs). He is eternal: He was there before the beginning, He created the beginning, He was, is and will be forever more. He IS.

2. Of the Bible – Every true thing we know about God, faith and salvation comes from the Bible. A new audience haven't read it, and don't know why it is inerrant, yet we ask them to abandon their lives on the basis of its call.

3. Of Man - Each of us was created and placed on the earth by design; not by an evolution accident, but intentionally by God. He knows even the thoughts and the number of hairs on the heads of eight plus billion people on the earth. We are accountable to God for how we live. From birth we are sinful and we cannot make ourselves good.

4. Of Time – There will be an end to time, and then comes eternity. We already live eternally, because even when our bodies die, our souls live on forever.

5. Of Destinations – We live on the earth in preparation for what comes. There are only two eternal destinations: a blissful heaven or a fearful hell. Everyone takes part.

6. <u>Of Christ</u> – God's Son, Jesus Christ, is God Himself. He was born into this world, through the conception by the Spirit of God. He lived without sin, was killed most cruelly, God then resurrected Him and returned Him to heaven, all by design! The reason for His earthly life? To show us the way to the Father and to die for our sins in our place to make the only way to the Father. At the Father's command He will come again.
7. <u>Of God's Love</u> – God loves all people deeply, to the extent that His Son died for us, whether we accept Him as our Lord and Saviour or not (*'This is love: not that we loved God, but that He loved us and sent His Son as an atoning sacrifice for our sins'* ***1 John 4:10***).
8. <u>Of Faith</u> – We don't benefit from His love unless we love Him back. To believe in Jesus is to abandon our lives and trust Him.
9. <u>Of Choices</u> – Our choices and earthly lives determine our eternity. Our purpose is not to live for our own pleasure, but for God's glory. Following Him in His way may even lead us to be separated from loved ones and friends.
10. <u>Of Judgement, Heaven and Hell</u> – There will be a Judgement Day at the end of time. Jesus will judge each person rightly. Only those who became children of God through faith in Jesus and remain in Him to the end will live with Him in heaven forever. All others, regardless of personal goodness, will be sent to an eternity in hell.

How do we get people to believe all this? We can't and we don't. But God can and does. He awakens hearts by different means: conviction of sin, a life crisis, the wonder of creation or the miracle of a new-born baby or questions about the sense of life and eternity. He may touch some people with the Gospel message even long before they understand a fraction of the wider truth, but when they do meet Him personally, they will accept the rest in time.

This is, of course, not only a faith challenge for someone who hears the Gospel message for the first time; it is also for each of us! But each of us is intrinsically wired with a God-given conscience, the ability to recognise Him in creation and to respond to Him (*'since what may be known about God is plain to them, because God has made it plain to them. For since the creation of the world God's invisible qualities—His eternal power and divine nature—have been clearly seen, being understood from what has been made, so that people are without excuse'* **Rom 1:19-20**).

As impossible and insurmountable as these challenges may seem, God can stir any heart to the truth of the Gospel. He is the one who draws us and He saves, not the evangelist. Giving a 'soft' message to accommodate the hearer does not help them! Only the truth of Christ, spoken in love, does. Let us proclaim the Gospel accurately and make disciples and leave it to God to bring conviction and grant salvation and eternal life. Nothing else will save them.

The Gospel demands a response, yet not all responses lead to salvation. Many aren't prepared for the cost of following, even if they generally subscribe to being a Christian.

Should we expect someone to develop a First Love relationship with Jesus after the briefest of introductions? If we don't expect that in human relationships, why do we expect it with the Gospel, which is far greater, more challenging and life-altering than human? People can continue in selfishness, pride and all manner of falsehood in a marriage, yet God does not allow this in the Bride of Christ. To lay down everything and develop a love relationship with Jesus does not happen overnight! Rather than a quick conversion we should expect a deeper path. Anything shorter will be the exception!

It is essential that we align with God's view of what happens when people say 'yes'. Only His view matters. Our evangelism will only be successful if the person's heart is chosen by God. God draws, yet we must yield and choose Jesus and then God sovereignly gives His grace and saves.

We must make disciples; God saves

And what about ourselves? Is it reasonable to think we were saved after we said 'yes' and were led in a sincere prayer? <u>Have we really passed God's 'Bride of Christ test'?</u>

'Come and See' – Decide if you can Follow Me!

Everyone in the church wants to go to heaven. If the cost is low enough, who wouldn't want to? Yet, what is on offer is not heaven, but Jesus! He is the prize and to follow Jesus and become one with Him has life-changing implications. Jesus commands that we calculate the cost before we start building our faith tower (**Luke 14:28**). At many outreaches there is an expectation of quick conversions. Yet expectations of early salvation come from the seeker but with the evangelist. The seeker will go where they are led. If someone will proclaim salvation over them, they are just too happy to accept it.

Most evangelists call an early pledge 'salvation'. It isn't!

When people are being promised salvation and heaven for saying a prayer, that does not change God's views or His ways. Until we truly want Jesus as our First Love, we remain outside the small gate. Salvation is God's sovereign gift of grace based on our response to Jesus. In the meantime we should understand that we only 'come and see' (***John 1:39-41***).

To say 'yes' to Jesus without a complete life change leaves us no better off than we were before. Years of service and sacrifice in the church are meaningless; whether as one in the audience, a worship leader or preacher for a lifetime, serving at a home church or abroad, being called 'Reverend', 'Pastor', 'Doctor' or 'Professor' with several theological PhD's, even the Pope or the greatest Christian apologist. The gate is the same width for everyone and all must find and enter in God's way.

Some refer to the 3,000 who were saved at hearing Peter's words in ***Acts 2*** and assume people are still being saved this way. Is it possible? Yes, with God all things are possible. Yet, these were the most unusual of circumstances. We cannot compare them directly with today's outreaches. Please read the account with an eye on the detail:

- These were religious Jews who grew up with a knowledge of God since their birth ('Men of Israel' ***v23***, 'Let all Israel be assured of this' ***v36***). They were knowledgeable about God, His laws and about the coming Messiah. Peter quoted ***Psalm 110:1*** and they recognised it.

- They already knew about the ministry of the man Jesus: His words, His claims to be the Son of God, that He is God and about His miracles.

- Many of them had seen Him in the flesh. They also knew He was killed; some may have witnessed His death on the cross. His death was fresh in everyone's mind.

- Peter told them they were part-responsible for Jesus' death. When they heard this, God opened their eyes to who Jesus was and to their guilt. Hence they cried out in Godly sorrow 'what must we do?' (***v37***). Now they 'believed in Jesus' because they realised His claims were true. Peter promised if they repented, they would receive the Spirit (*v38*), which they did.

How can this account be compared with what we see at modern Gospel meetings or programmes? We cannot expect salvation to come to the majority and so quickly.

There is also the Criminal on the Cross example we discussed in Book 1. Our theology cannot be based on this one example of God's most spectacular mercy, in the most unique of circumstances in history, and expect the same from our own outreaches! His example shows that there is hope in God's mercy right to the end, not that God applies different measures to different people.

Jesus says 'ask, seek, and knock'. 'Come and find out more about Me. See who I am and what I expect of you. Decide if you can follow Me. Are you prepared for the cost: losing your life, obedience and persecution, to put everything second to Me?' What Jesus expects of us is the opposite of human nature. Why do we expect all this to happen after a single prayer? Even when people are cut to the heart over their sinfulness, if they don't change for the rest of their lives, nothing changed. Today's tears and sincerity are not the salvation of tomorrow.

The truth of our faith depends on if we 'come and see' and follow. If not, we will simply say 'yes' to what we don't grasp and will not be nearer salvation, regardless of our confession.

Somehow many in the church don't understand or won't accept that Jesus will only be First in our lives. There are endless theological debates, arguments, petitions, new church movements, trends, research, speakers, conferences, books and ideas, each defending its own organisations, traditions, views and interpretations of what they approve or disapprove of. Yet, in the end, only God's view matters. We must find out what He wants. Every other view and pursuit is meaningless.

A life of semi-surrender, lukewarm love, partial obedience and commitment is wasted. Our reasonable service and sincere intentions have no value before God

'Come and see' may be a lengthy journey and Jesus says that the majority of those who decide to follow, even closely, will never enter (*'I never knew you'*). Gospel programmes tend to be very light on Godly sorrow, true repentance and the cost of discipleship. Yet, if God will not approve without these, why exclude these essentials?

The church must be more circumspect about leading people through 'come and see'.

Let us bring followers into the church, but not pronounce salvation over them for their decision

Let us disciple those in the church Biblically, to the point that God confirms their faith. Until then, they are not a part of God's family, even if they are in the 'church family'.

Like Jesus we should encourage people to follow, *'teaching them to obey everything I have commanded you'* (**_Mat 28:20_**). There are outreach programmes where, even after the shortest introduction to the programme, people are already asked if they want to give their lives to Jesus. This is even without talking about sin and repentance and the cost of following. Everyone is asked to keep their heads down and eyes shut so as not to embarrass the person who responds. IS THIS HOW WE LEAD OTHERS TO FOLLOW THE SAVIOUR? Without repentance? Not wanting to embarrass them?

In Jesus' time many followed Him for reasons other than that he was the Messiah: a fascination with the supernatural, miraculous food, healings, wise teachings, even for opposing the religious leaders. Most came with eyes fixed on the present world, not on the Author of Life. This is still the case today. If we really love the lost, then we must guard against these spiritual rabbit trails and help them find true salvation.

Jesus is our example. He said *'Foxes have dens and birds have nests, but the Son of Man has no place to lay His head'* (**Mat 8:20**). He entered the world with nothing, owned little but had use of everything He needed, His great treasure was His relationship with His Father. He lived to love and serve others, and died leaving everything behind, knowing His life was in heaven. He is our example – this world is not our home!

Let us 'Come and See' if we want to follow and encourage others to do the same. <u>Even after 50 years as a professing Christian we may still not have embraced the cost of following.</u>

The Fear of God

'The fear of God is the beginning of all wisdom' (**Prov 9:10**).

The fear of God is deep reverence for the Almighty God, for His holiness and understanding there will be a Judgement when we will be called to account. The fear of God is indeed the beginning of all wisdom, because it teaches us what is eternal and what matters. This leads us to the truth of Christ.

I believe it should be core to our prayers in churches and for evangelism that God will awaken hearts to who He is. It is crucial for Godly sorrow and repentance, without which there is no salvation. It is also core to understanding why obedience is so essential in the life of the true child of God.

The modern church has a terminal lack of reverence and fear of God. We approach God so casually. It has swung so far towards God's love and hyper-grace that God is almost a play-friend rather than God Almighty. One children's song even says 'He's my mate'. This screams to heaven! Take heed of the warning of **Psalm 50:21** (NLT) *'While you did all this, I remained silent, and you thought I didn't care. But now I will rebuke you, listing all My charges against you.'*

We cannot profess to revere God, yet pay lip service to His Word. There is no difference between God and His Word – they are One. Until we regain and preach reverence for and fear of God and His Word (*'tremble at His word'* **Is 66:2,5**), our evangelistic efforts outside the church and pastoral efforts within the church will remain powerless, ineffective and without fruit. We may gain converts but salvation will remain sadly absent. If you do not have a fear of God, ask Him to reveal Himself so your faith will have the Object of the Holy God.

Godly Sorrow

'Godly sorrow brings repentance that leads to salvation and leaves no regret, but worldly sorrow brings death' (**2 Cor 7:10**).

There is no shortcut to salvation. True salvation always begins with why I desperately need the Saviour. Until then, all my faith, my efforts and service and my life of restraint and piety, are wasted. There is no point in hearing we are sinful and that Jesus died for our sins and going through the motions of repentance. We must know our sinfulness at the depth of our being, painfully and gut-wrenchingly.

<u>Worldly sorrow</u> results from being confronted with the earthly consequences of our actions for ourselves or others. Contrition, regret and remorse are emotions towards humans, including ourselves, but not God. There is an impenetrable hard shell that will not recognise our sinfulness before God.

We don't need 'godly sorrow' but 'Godly sorrow', seeing ourselves through God's eyes

<u>Godly sorrow</u> comes from a <u>God-given</u> knowledge of our depravity before Him. We cannot self-generate this insight, nor the scope of our sinfulness. This is the gift of God. I must realise, by God's mercy, that there is nothing good in me and that I have no merit before Him.

Some may come to the Gospel already touched by God with sorrow over their sinfulness – like the woman who washed Jesus' feet with her tears and dried them with her hair (**<u>Luke 7:36-50</u>**). They only need to hear the Gospel and of God's love and grace and they move on rapidly towards salvation in Christ. Some may experience a life event where God is clearly at work, like the jailer of **<u>Acts 16:30</u>** *'Sirs what must I do to be saved?'* Others may hear the Gospel, fall under God's conviction with fear and sorrow as in **<u>Acts 2:37</u>** (*'When the people heard this, they were cut to the heart and said to Peter and the other apostles, "Brothers, what shall we do?"'*.

Unfortunately, the vast majority who 'decide for Christ' have no concept of their sinfulness; therefore their interest in the Gospel is only for assurance of heaven. This misses the point of salvation by a country mile! Much can be traced back to our evangelism: we are trying to save people from hell and make Christians who go to heaven. God wants worshippers of Jesus and reborn children who mourn their depravity and want only Jesus because of His sacrifice for them.

I am concerned by outreaches that do not encourage time for deep reflection before God. Commitments to Jesus based on anything other than Godly sorrow are shallow and certainly not salvation. Why a Saviour if we don't realise how sinful we are? This revelation is a gift from a loving God. Why not ask

Him for this insight? Why is it not core to our Gospel message and a key prayer in preparation for our evangelism that God will reveal each person's sorrowful state?

Tears of sorrow are the mark of God turning up! There is either sorrow in this life or wailing forever in the next. Salvation does not start with believing in Jesus, but with realising how sinful **I** am. **I** am utterly lost and **I** need the Saviour. The death of Jesus is meaningless until **I** realise **I** am the one He died for because **I** am sinful and **I** am going to hell!

Unless I have been broken before God about my own sinfulness, there is no true repentance and therefore no life. Only then will I sing with the hymn 'Rock of Ages':

Nothing in my hand I bring,
Simply to Thy cross I cling;
Naked, come to Thee for dress;
Helpless, look to Thee for grace;
Foul, I to the fountain fly;
Wash me, Saviour, or I die.

If I am not desperate to be washed of my sins, I will not bow to a Lord. I don't receive a Saviour because I want heaven, I receive Him because I am desperate to be cleansed!

We have nothing to give to God and no merit before Him. He sees the scarlet of my sinfulness, not the goodness I think of myself or that others may perceive. It is terrible before God that may I think I can have anything good to offer Him, to compete with Christ. If we could offer something good, would God not rather have accepted that than punish His Son?

No, God accepts only one goodness: Christ Jesus.

Unless I come before the Father, with a shredded heart, depending on His mercy on the basis of His Son, there is no hope for me. '*Nothing in my hand I bring, simply to the cross*

I cling ... Wash me, Saviour, or I'll die' indeed! Nothing good lives in me (**Rom 7:18**).

Godly sorrow is not for the proud but for those on their faces before God. *'Blessed are those who mourn, for they will be comforted'* (**Mat 5:3**).

Why are there so few on the narrow road? It starts right here – do I ask God to show me my true condition and to break me over my sinfulness, regardless of the cost? Only then will it make sense to hear *'Though your sins are like scarlet, they shall be as white as snow; though they are red as crimson, they shall be like wool'* (**Is 1:18**).

Godly sorrow does not guarantee salvation but true salvation always starts with Godly sorrow. It is the deep soil in which repentance grows. This is why, in the Parable of the Sower, the plant in the rocky soil dies. It's root isn't in the depth of Godly sorrow and repentance.

If you haven't yet experienced Godly sorrow, ask God. Don't be in a hurry to get past this point. Remain in the dark before God for as long as it takes.

Repentance and Obedience

'Godly sorrow leads to repentance that leads to life'. Godly sorrow, repentance and life are indispensable links in an unbroken chain. As Godly sorrow is essential for repentance, so repentance is essential for 'life'. Repentance and obedience are two sides of the same coin. We repent of what must not be and turn to Christ to obey Him in what He requires.

<u>Repentance</u>

It bears repeating because there is such a disconnect in our churches on this Godly truth: There is no salvation without true repentance. True repentance is the turning point. We went in one direction, sinful, proud, disobedient, self-focused, and now we turn to go towards Jesus and His ways and words.

What is the meaning of repentance? To give up our sinful ways, lament, be sorrowful, be ashamed of, be contrite AND amend our ways by coming to Jesus and turn to His ways! This true turning away will not happen unless we are cut to the heart about our sinfulness in Godly sorrow, hence *'Godly sorrow leads to repentance that leads to life'*.

The importance of repentance for salvation is very clear:

- John the Baptist preached repentance (*'In those days John the Baptist came, preaching in the wilderness of Judea and saying, "<u>Repent</u>, for the kingdom of heaven has come near"'* **Mat 3:1-2**).
- The first recorded word of Jesus' ministry was *'Repent!'* (**Mat 4:17**, **Mark 1:15**)
- The first message the 12 apostles preached when they were sent out by Jesus was *'Repent'* (**Mark 6:12**),
- The first word in Peter's first recorded sermon in Acts was *'Repent'* (**Acts 2: 38**); and
- Paul said God had commanded all men everywhere to <u>repent</u> (**Acts 17:30**).
- <u>Repentance</u> is a central theme of the Bible when God gave people the opportunity to turn to Him.

Repentance is central to the Gospel. It doesn't mean I begin to be greatly influenced by Jesus, or that I reform a lot of my ways. The literal translation of the Greek *'metanoia'* is 'a new (change of) mind'. Yet it isn't to change my mind superficially but in a deep sense due to realising my sinfulness, who Jesus is and His authority as the Son of God.

I often hear it said that we must just change our minds about Jesus. Yet it is totally without merit if it does not bring radical life and deep-heart change! It is a fallacy to think I can change my mind without radically changing my ways! True repentance, obedience, surrender and love are all parts of the same life-change!

Repentance that God accepts comes without explanations or preconditions. To say 'I am sorry I did that, but he made me angry' is a justification, not even an apology, and certainly not repentance! I pretend I'm sorry, but blame someone else. Humans may accept that but not God – we still hold out in pride and self-righteousness. We either come in repentance or we stay in our sins, regardless of our words and tears.

It is Biblically impossible to be the same after repentance than before! I cannot claim repentance and still have the same independence, selfishness, aspirations, petulance, ambition, fears, pride, anger, easy offense and unforgiveness and. If we do, then know for sure repentance never happened!

So, what must I change my mind about?

Firstly, a God-given realisation that nothing good lives in me (**_Rom 7:18_**) and I am sinful. I even repent of my good works for thinking they make me good in God's eyes - *'all our righteous acts are like filthy rags'* (**_Is 64:6_**).

Secondly, I realise Jesus, who is Himself God (**_John 8:58_**), died for my depravity because God hates sin (*'But God shows His love for us in that while we were still sinners, Christ died for us'* **_Rom 5:8_**).

Thirdly, as Lord He commands what He expects of His followers (*'Why do you call Me "Lord, Lord" and do not do what I say?'* **_Luke 6:46_**). Obedience confirms my decision to follow Jesus. If I claim His name, there is only His way.

Fourthly, He is worthy and demands that I relinquish my life to Him ('*In the same way, those of you who do not give up everything you have cannot be My disciples*' **Luke 14:33**).

Fifthly, to stop sinning ('*See, you are well again. Stop sinning or something worse may happen to you*' **John 5:14**). If I claim to follow Jesus, then I must address known wilful, careless sins with utter resolve and put resolute checks in place so I don't return to them, even though I may fail again.

Lastly, I realise He will only accept being my First Love ('*Anyone who loves their father or mother more than Me is not worthy of Me; anyone who loves their son or daughter more than Me is not worthy of Me*' **Mat 10:37**).

---

*Jesus is Lord (**Mat 28:18**), whether I accept it or not. I must place myself under Him purposely, permanently*

Repentance in the full Christian context is to agree with, obey and prefer everything Jesus said: deny myself, die to myself, give up everything. Only at this point have I 'changed my mind'. This is my on-going state of heart before God for the rest of my days – a repentant life.

Salvation is not a 'Christian' right. I don't cast token faith at Jesus and get saved. I am under no obligation to follow Him and He is under no obligation to accept me. He has mercy on who He has mercy (**Rom 9:15**) and we are only saved by His grace. We can call ourselves born-again but we don't get to choose His best and ignore His preconditions.

We close this discussion: <u>Without repentance there is no reconciliation with God</u>. Some think repentance can come after salvation, but that is un-Biblical: Repentance is central to salvation; my choices flow out of conviction. God judges if my repentance is real or not. Let us preach true repentance before we encourage people to make a commitment to follow!

Obedience

The true disciple of Jesus does what He did and said. That is what a disciple is! In the same way repentance and obedience are linked, there is only a hair's difference between obedience and faith. The Bible sometimes uses them inter-changeably: *"Whoever believes in the Son has eternal life; whoever does not obey the Son shall not see life"* (***John 3: 36*** ESV). Likewise love for Jesus and obedience are linked: Those who obey are the ones who love Jesus (***John 14:21***) and those who love are the ones who obey (***John 14:15,23***). It is spiritual circular breathing!

There are around 20 passages just from the mouth of Jesus, and a similar number from the rest of the New Testament writers, on obedience and faith, love and salvation.

Is obedience optional? Or is it core to saving faith? Judge for yourself: '*For whoever does the will of My Father in heaven is My brother and sister and mother*' (***Mat 12:50***). '*And teaching them to obey everything that I commanded you*' (***Mat 28:20***). '*For whoever does the will of God is My brother and sister and mother*' (***Mark 3:35***). '*Why do you call Me Lord, Lord and don't do what I say?*' (***Luke 6:46***). *You are My friends if you do what I command*' (***John 15:14***). There are many more. '*... He became the source of eternal salvation for all who obey Him*' (***Heb 5:8-9***). '*This is how we know that we love the children of God: by loving God and carrying out His commandments. This is love for God: to obey His commandments*' (***1 John 5:2-5***). '*And this is love: that we walk in obedience to His commands...*' (***2 John v6***).

It is madness and false teaching to disconnect obedience from our saved status. Yet understand this: obedience is never the way to salvation, but always the evidence of hearts that really seek Him and of those who are saved. Can I ignore obedience when I seek Jesus? What do you think?

> *Teaching on obedience and repentance is virtually absent in the entire church today*

These words on the importance of obedience are the actual commands of Jesus Himself, yet somehow doing what Jesus commanded is now considered 'salvation by works'. **Since when is it works to do what God says?** Is it works to take Jesus at His word in faith and to act upon it, works to forgive, to stop sinning, to give up everything we have to find this Great Treasure of God? We have become so grace obsessed that we are willing to oppose Jesus to His face rather than obey Him, all in the name of easy grace. It just shows the true state of our hearts – we never intended to have Him as Lord, because we never thought we were so sinful in the first place!

Start obeying when you begin to follow and continue lifelong! We are to take His words seriously and teach others the same (**Mat 28:20**).

My observation about obedience is that everyone in the church applauds 'faith in Jesus', but the divide comes when someone actually starts to obey (or preaches that we should). The emphasis on grace is the escape route for those with little intention to obey and don't want to teach it either. In contrast, those outside the church expect professing believers to obey the Bible and take issue when Christians don't!

The upshot is a strange phenomenon: those outside the church don't believe, but see obedience as a logical, integral part of the Christian. Inside the church we profess to believe, but take a relaxed view of obedience, that it isn't essential.

The only conclusion that can be drawn is that the two groups have the same worldly nature: the religious inside the church profess a faith but have no intention to obey their professed Lord; those outside the church disobey anyway but don't make excuses for their sin. This is consistent with the word of Jesus – both groups are unsaved!

Obedience is the outflow of heart-level abandon. To put it crudely: someone may only just have started their journey and perhaps only 'obey 1%' but they have already surrendered their hearts in full and God accepts them. Others may 'obey 95%' (legalistically) but hang onto the true loves of their lives. They haven't surrendered to Jesus. Obedience is a heart thing, not a legalistic precondition! When we come to Him, we hand over control. Nothing else pleases the Father.

The key to salvation is not what we think *'believe'* in **_John 3:16_** is, but how that faith expresses itself in love and obedience (**_John 14:15-24_**). When it is our heart's desire to do what He wants, then *'My Father will love him and We will come to him and make Our home with him'*.

---

*Jesus said and did exactly what the Father told Him (**_John 5:19_**, **_12:49_**). This was how He showed He loved the Father. He uses the same measure for us*

Obedience is NOT optional! *Jesus says so!*

We will not find Jesus unless we take His seriously as Lord. If we say we follow, then follow as Jesus requires – doing what He commands. Read His words intentionally. [An excellent resource, *The John 7:17 Challenge* by Michael Chriswell (available only at relentlessheart.com) explains 90 teachable commands of Jesus (with audio).]

Learn About, Believe and Trust in Jesus

In any relationship knowledge of the other person is essential for lasting union. Infatuation may bring instant connection but it isn't a basis for lasting love. With Jesus it's about getting to know the One we will spend all eternity with.

<u>Learn About Jesus</u>

Faith in Jesus consists of much more than the facts about His life on earth and that He died for our sins. Some of these are: He existed before creation and always existed with the Father (***John 1:1***). He is one with the Father (***John 10:30***) and He is God (***John 1:18)***. All things were made by Him and for Him (***John 1:3***, ***Col 1:16***). He is the Christ (***Mat 16:16***), the Messiah (***Mat 1:16***). All authority in heaven and earth belongs to Him (***Mat 28:18***). He comes again, will reign on the earth for 1,000 years (mentioned seven times in ***Rev 20:2-7***) and will judge the living and the dead (***2 Tim 4:1***).

Furthermore, Jesus confirmed the Old Testament by quoting from it. He confirmed events and people, e.g. creation, Noah, Lot's wife and Sodom and Gomorrah, Jonah, the prophets from Abel to Zechariah and the moral Law. His own birth, life, death, resurrection and second coming are the fulfilment of a great number of Old Testament prophecies from Old Testament books spanning Genesis (the first book) to Malachi (the last book). Believing in Jesus, therefore, also means faith in all of Scripture, including the Old Testament.

Faith in Jesus includes to learn and live what He taught

Jesus cannot be separated from His words. His words express His and the Father's heart and what it means to follow

Him. Therefore, faith in Him demands faith in His second coming, in the Day of Judgement and in heaven and hell (and its severity!) and who He says will go to each.

Do we need to know everything, from Genesis to Revelation and about Jesus, before salvation? Obviously not. Yet certain facts are core to believing in Him. If we cannot live with the facts, we cannot live with Him. True faith in Jesus requires a teachable spirit and a heart <u>already</u> committed to Jesus. Such a heart will embrace Bible truths about Christ as and when God reveals it by His Spirit.

<u>Believe and Trust in Jesus (Human-level Faith)</u>

It takes <u>faith to act</u> on the beliefs we profess so easily! Faith is belief that I am prepared to act on

Faith in Christ has considerable implications! The greater the potential cost of failure, the more faith is required. Any faith that does not act, is not true faith. To say I believe in Jesus, but I am not convinced or compelled to act, puts into question my professed faith. It takes faith to rely and act on God's words when it makes no sense in the natural. Not to worry but to live trusting in God requires faith, as does to choose God's will over my natural desires and loves.

Scripture says *'without faith it is impossible to please God, because anyone who comes to Him must believe that He exists and that He rewards those who earnestly seek Him'* (**Heb 11:6**). Ultimately only the faith which Jesus authors satisfies God. Yet, God requires that we first step out in our human faith on what He commands. It is active, working faith, rather than intellectual, passive faith, that pleases Him.

Until we meet Jesus, we only have human-level faith. This requires the 'risk' to trust Him and His words and to override our human fear, reluctance and rebellion. We don't do it blindly, but we face the facts and choose to believe God over our circumstances, loves and fears. If we don't, we will be like Jesus' followers who saw so many miracles, yet failed to believe in Him. How strange that we criticise the faith of the Jews for not believing Jesus, yet that is what happens in our churches today – Christian atheism!

God wants to see us step out and trust Him. He will test us increasingly for greater acts of faith. It will challenge us even when we have seen Him come through miraculously before. Every new situation requires a new day's faith. It develops our relationship with God when we see Him act in ways we never imagined. This process continues lifelong.

Our deepest faith shows, not when we trust God for a specific outcome, but when we entrust Him with the outcome, even if it may cost us dearly

---

When we trust God regardless of outcome we rest in His sovereignty, goodness and righteousness and that He knows best. This is why Paul said in **Romans 8:28** 'And we know that in all things God works for the good of those who love Him, who have been called according to His purpose'.

If only we would believe from the outset that God is absolutely trustworthy and that we can let go and trust Him. How much quicker will we not get to where God wants us to be! If we will relinquish life and cast ourselves on Him our use in His hands will grow exponentially.

Our final point about human faith is found in **John 12:42-50**. Many amongst the leaders believed in Jesus, yet, due to their fear of the Pharisees they would not openly confess their faith 'because they loved praise from men more than *praise from God'* (v43). The modern church would say these Pharisees are saved because 'they believed in Jesus'. How then should we judge this scenario? **John 12:25** gives the answer *'Anyone who loves their life will lose it, while anyone who hates their life in this world will keep it for eternal life'*. And **Luke 14:26** reads *'If anyone comes to Me and does not hate father and mother, wife and children, brothers and sisters – yes, even their own life – such a person cannot be My disciple'*. These Pharisees may have believed in Jesus, but they valued their earthly lives more. He was not their Lord, nor did they consider Him of greater value than their earthly lives. Jesus said they would surely not inherit the kingdom of God. Neither will we if we do the same.

In contrast to human faith, which is our definite act of trust, saving faith 'fizzes out' from our hearts once we have met Jesus. The memory of the Spirit rebirthing us is what we recall to the end of our days. This testimony of the Spirit and His presence strengthen me as I step out in trust and He makes possible faith acts and outcomes I could never imagine or do on my own. This includes suffering for Jesus in the face of great adversity. I step out in trepidation, trusting in God, and He makes my steps firm with the certainty and confidence of Hebrews 11:1. Then God does through me what only He can.

Faith in the truth is profitable. Believing in a lie or a half-truth is useless, even if everyone believes the same

---

It is pointless to believe God for something that is inconsistent with His Word, even if it wins the admiration of others. We must build our lives on the correct beliefs.

Lose My Life (Die to Myself), Surrender to Christ

Our journey to salvation is still on the wide road outside the small, narrow Gate of Jesus, even if it may be very near.

Lose my life

> *'He is no fool who gives up what he cannot keep, to gain what he cannot lose'* - Jim Elliot

Jesus makes 'losing my life' a precondition of being His (true, saved) disciple (*'For whoever wants to save their life will lose it, but whoever loses their life for Me will find it'* **Mat 16:25**). This is only possible if we value Jesus higher than our earthly lives, or we will have no incentive. We cannot achieve this on our own though; instead we must ask Jesus to help us. I found out this truth way too late!

What does it mean to lose my life?

Firstly, for the vast majority it will not mean losing their physical life.

Secondly, it rather means to place on the altar all my loves and what defines my life and to set aside my own priorities, for the sake of following Jesus and putting His priorities and commands first. Does this mean waving goodbye to my life of family, work and other elements? It may, if that life conflicts with following Christ, e.g. if I make a living by illegal means. More likely it means giving up the priority I give to my own status, comfort, loves, material wealth, etc. It includes giving up self-seeking behaviour such as pride, easy offense, jealousy, anger, dependencies and attention and approval-seeking, etc.

Thirdly, perhaps at a more mature stage of my following, it will be a willing choice to 'put to death' legitimate desires to pursue the separated and contented life in Christ. We don't have to guess what to do though, God will make it known to us.

The consequence of full surrender is that I no longer decide my life; I follow where Jesus leads me. This 'lost life' becomes indefensible to others, even to professing Christians; people who want to control their lives and want to know your life plans, future, career decisions and retirement plans. Yet when you truly lose your life you become a part of God's plan. God takes care of you and He does not reveal His plans fully upfront! You live in a different economy: there is abundance even when in the natural there is only a dry desert or a stony riverbed. You don't need proof before you step out on God's promises because you know He will take care of the details.

Giving Up

In much of our evangelism people say Jesus is knocking on your door but the handle is on the inside, and quote **Revelation 3: 20** out of context. They say He wants to come in and make His home with you if you will just let Him in. This makes us think He will make our earthly lives better. We will do better when we understand Jesus called *'Follow Me'* (**Mat 4:19**) and *'Come to Me'* (**Mat 11:28**). He calls us out, away from our lives. There is no salvation where we are in our sins and our worldly attachments. *'Without holiness no-one will see God'* (**Heb 12:14**). We must come away if to find Him.

We lose our lives (and die to ourselves). That leaves only one life to live – Jesus. We cannot add Jesus' holiness to what we have. He meets us outside our own camp, as God did with Moses. We cast our lives aside and move to Him before He is in us. He says *'My yoke is easy and My burden is light'* (**Mat 11:30**). In order to get His easy yoke and light burden, I lay down my own heavy burden and my own hard yoke of choice outside the gate. He will not help me carry or improve the earthly life I collect, strain under and refuse to let go of: earthly comfort in the good life, materialism, dreams of a better life, sins, worldly passions and expectations, wrong relationships, unholy lifestyles, unforgiveness, ambitions and selfish desires, pride and even fears and worries – I must give all that up.

How we mess up our lives and the lives of others with anger, sexual promiscuity, greed, selfishness! Then we ask Jesus to bless the toxic, the sinful, the lifestyle, the beliefs. His purpose is set us free from all that. We cannot become one with Him while we cling onto weeds, dross, sin and filth in our lives. We cannot trade favours by putting down individual things in return for His blessings. We have nothing God wants! No, He says, 'Let it all go, or you may ultimately as well stay as you are and abandon Me in total – there is no eternal difference'.

When God requires me to give up, we don't just promise to in the future so we can go to heaven. It must happen at heart-level now. Some think Jesus saves us and we walk on the narrow road, still hanging onto our sinful attachments, saved but slowly shed our sins at our discretion. No, if we really met Jesus, the old will go because sin is against the Spirit's nature.

Our pastoral teams are being overrun: we hope people will get better if we wait long enough and they keep following. Yet most don't, because they never renounced sin; they are still on the broad road. We allow them to think they can be saved with all the stuff and so we cement in their unbelief and error.

'For whoever wants to save their life will lose it, but whoever loses their life for Me will save it'. These words appear four times in the Gospels: **Matthew 10:39**, **16:25**, **Mark 8:35** and **Luke 9:24**. It is almost like Jesus meant what He said! *'Those of you who do not give up everything you have cannot be My disciples'* (**Luke 14:33**).

Jesus tells us what makes the gate so small and will stop us from entering in. Amongst others:

- If we love anyone more than Him, we are not worthy of Him (**_Mat 10:37_**).
- If we don't give up everything we have, we cannot be His disciple (**_Luke 14:33_**).
- If we don't hate (in comparison with our First Love for Jesus) all other people and even our own lives, we cannot be His disciple **_(Luke 14:26_**).
- If we don't pick up our cross and follow Him (**_Mat 10:38_**)
- If we don't lose our lives and find it in Christ (**_Mat 10:39_**).
- If we don't deny ourselves (**_Luke 9:23_**).
- If we don't hold to His teachings and commandments ('*If you hold to My teachings you are really My disciple*' **_John 8:31_**).

Do I fear what God may ask me to give up or take away if I hand it over? That is the first indication that I love something more than Jesus. I know people who insist they don't get angry. And yet everyone knows they do! They don't scream and shout, but in slow-burning anger they get even, one way or another.

Can we pray with a clear conscience 'Lord show me whatever stands between me and You and I will give it up'? Am I prepared to plead with God to remove anything that competes with Him? And when He does, will I give it up gladly, or will God have to pry it out of my hands to save me from myself? Is there a treasure I will not entrust to God? My loved ones, my emotions, money, loves, good looks, stuff, addictions, prejudices, pride, past hurts?

Can we truly say *'I consider everything a loss because of the surpassing worth of knowing Christ Jesus my Lord, for whose sake I have lost all things'* (**Phil 3:8**)?

Can we really say we will do whatever, sell and give away whatever, be humiliated however, as long as we obtain Jesus, our Lord, because He is indeed worth everything to us?

Jesus gives us His burden and His yoke once we give up ours. Now we have a new perspective on what is of true and lasting value. These are the *'good gifts'* of God (**Mat 7:11**). Now our requests will reflect God's priorities rather than the burdens and yokes of a selfish life with Satan as our father.

Is the earthly burden easy to shed? No! This is where the pain is - 'agónizomai' (agonise) to enter

---

Again, God does not expect us to lose every part of our lives before He lets us in, but He wants us to set lives down at heart-level. The detail of individual things will come later, on the narrow road (sanctification). But often there are things that we refuse bluntly to let go of. That leaves us outside the gate, even if we laid down all else. Once laid down, it makes for light travelling on the narrow road that follows.

Surrender to Christ

We must surrender our lives to Christ. Dietrich Bonhoeffer said *'When Christ calls a man, He bids him come and die'* – the death of our old nature. That nature must die before the new nature can live; the two will not co-exist. In part we must bring it to an end, and in part God will bring it to an end. Here we discuss what we must do.

'In the same way, those of you who do not give up everything you have cannot be My disciples' (**Luke 14:33**).

It sounds as if it's just about possessions, until we look at the original. The intention is much wider: it is my own 'I am', my core 'go to', whatever captivates me, my personhood, my own 'beginning and end' and existence. It is the opposite of what I possess, but rather what possesses me. My appearance, loves, intellect, hates, what I take pride in, shame, aspirations, lusts, unforgiveness, comforts, what holds my thoughts. And yes, stuff also! In short: that which defines me. This is what I must give up. It is so serious. Perhaps just one thing keeps me hell-bound because I refuse to let go of 'me'. We either renounce our old lives now, or we will be confronted at the Judgement when it is too late.

Life of Dedication v Life of Surrender

Earlier we have touched on this briefly but I create a special sub-heading for this discussion because the distinction is subtle but all-important: there is a world of difference between dedicating my life to Christ and surrendering to Him. The difference is who decides my life, therefore who is Lord. It is all-important for our salvation.

To live a life of dedication is to be sincere in what I do for Christ, yet I decide what is being done. I know people who decide to give up a year or more for Jesus, to do His work, believing it shows their love and dedication for Him. They do things <u>for Him</u>. Yet it is an expression of my religion and I decide the nature of my dedication. This can lead to a very active church, faith and charitable life and even self-martyrdom, which may appear very pious. Yet we justify our own faith and how we express it.

To surrender is the complete opposite. Paul says '*I have been crucified with Christ and I no longer live, but Christ lives in me. The life I now live in the body, I live by faith in the Son of God, who loved me and gave Himself for me*' (**<u>Gal 2:20</u>**). I die to myself and therefore Christ lives through me. He may leave me 'on the shelf' for a long time while He refines me and uses me only in a single flash, which accomplishes far more than daily efforts over many years. Or He may do the opposite. But one thing is certain: He has complete Lordship over my life because I have surrendered my life entirely to Him. This choice to surrender is mine to make. I can believe in Jesus as much as I am able, yet unless this exchange has taken place at the heart level, then I am still lord. Only when Jesus lives through me does God glorify Himself through my life.

Our lives of dedication may achieve much in the church, but in eternal terms it not only won't achieve anything. We may also live the life of the religious Christian yet unrebirthed.

Jesus doesn't live in our lives; we live in His

Let us consider further how this truth may play out in our lives of faith:

Not only do we give up our lives <u>to</u> Christ, but also surrender the lives we decide to live <u>for</u> Christ – our hopes of what it means to live for Him. We may already have decided how we want to serve and we steer our ministry towards that. (Sadly, some others have no desire to serve God at all, they just want to be 'good Christians' and turn up on Sundays!)

Some have dreams of serving as a medical doctor on the mission field, others as a worship leader, others decide they want to go into or remain in business to make money so they can give, some want to serve in administration or a service where they feel comfortable and many more. Some are good speakers and so are drawn to preaching, others to leadership. Many are found in full-time ministry. These are all laudable but they appeal to our independent spirit, coated in our own charity 'I am doing this for God.' Yet this could be the same as an unbeliever with the same charitable passions.

God can use us in exactly the way we had hoped, but often He takes us through deep trials so we are first cured of our self-rule before we are fit for His service.

We must be careful of thinking we are doing something for Christ. Our choices may already hide our pride in what we do well, or where we want accolades in the earthly church, or what we are prepared to do for Jesus, on our own terms. This is not what Jesus wants. He demands our full allegiance, even in how we serve, even if in worldly terms we do that exceptionally well! Likewise, if you have been entrusted with much money, you must still seek Jesus first or all of your giving may be meaningless in eternal terms.

It is often said 'God does not call the equipped, but He equips the called'

To make our own choice of service is to act unilaterally, without knowledge of where God wants to use us. Don't get ahead of Him and decide how He must use you. He decides.

Professing Christians also have a tendency to pursue their own choice of career and life and fit church (Jesus?) into it. Few really lay down their lives and ask for God's will, but rather want Him to confirm what they already desire, which may include their own choice of service in the church or in Christian organisations or charities. Or they want God to help remove their uncertainty between choices they already assembled. Church (Jesus?) is an add-on to what they choose to do, rather than Jesus being the main driver in their lives. And once they achieve their goals or establish financial independence, they may offer some of their time to the church as an acceptable act of service. This must often fit in around interests, travel plans, care for grandchildren or elderly parents, etc. This is not forsaking the earthly life, but an ongoing pattern that has ruled their old lives of independence and personal lordship. This is no different from saying *"Lord, Lord', did we not ... in Your name?"* We decide what to do independently and expect God to merit our service.

Two lives may look exactly alike from the outside in terms of work, home, life and involvement in church and ministry. Yet for the one it may be what God ordained, and for the other not. God may want the one to be earning in order to give and the other to give up those things to serve Him in other ways. Each must listen for God's voice and not assume education, natural strengths, personal desires or professional aspirations for how to conduct our lives. Yet, before He will guide us, God expects obedience to what He has already said in His Word!

God does not want our leftovers once we have satisfied ourselves in the world, have a nest egg or are tired of doing our normal thing. True abandon is the opposite of what the world does and it invariably costs us in the natural. Sadly, to give up and forego is also the opposite of what most Christians will do.

Some forsake their lives quite early on. Others take a long time as they are being challenged with what they hold dear. The majority never give it up. God is not looking to see if we have given up every individual thing, but He judges our heart condition. Once that is settled, it is almost a formality to deal with actual issues because the heart is already won. The flipside is also true though: many proudly say they have given up their lives but in reality they haven't.

How do we know if we have fully surrendered? Firstly, God confirms us by His Spirit. Secondly, He wants a lifelong heart submission, so it should not matter to us whether we think we have given up 'enough' to be acceptable. Thirdly, ask

Him if anything hinders His work in you, anything that captivates you. God will test us. Be vigilant, and submit to everything He brings to mind. They will be things we resist naturally and it can be all too easy to brush it off when we are confronted. Whatever you do, though, deal with it determinedly, in a way that will last a lifetime.

You may argue along with the Many that Jesus never meant you must give up your whole life to Him. You just want to be a good Christian. But that is exactly what He expects. It is to part with all my rights and attachments to the worldly life, its loves and its trappings. And then He places you where He wants you. Perhaps He leaves you where you are, perhaps He moves you decisively away from where you are.

Deny Myself, Pick Up My Cross and Follow

Jesus said in **Luke 9:23** *'Whoever wants to be My disciple must deny themselves and take up their cross daily and follow Me'*. This is pretty clear: if we want to be His disciple, we <u>must</u> deny ourselves and pick up our cross <u>before we are let in through the narrow gate</u>. It is not optional. Denying ourselves and picking up our cross are not only components of discipleship after we are saved; we cannot be a true disciple in any other way. Or, to put it another way: We cannot be a part of the Few unless we deny ourselves, pick up our cross and follow Jesus. It starts outside the gate and continues lifelong!

<u>Deny myself</u>

To deny myself at the most basic level means leaving legitimate or good activity or life behind when God calls in a different direction. To deny myself includes refusing to act when I am justified in the world's eyes to take action but God calls me to give up my natural 'right' in obedience to Him. I may be justified in taking revenge or legal action for an offense against my person, yet God may command me to set it down to develop mercy and grace in me or to show His mercy to others through me. <u>Be assured, to deny yourself is the opposite of what the world would do.</u> Expect opposition, even from Christians.

<u>Pick up my Cross</u>

Picking up my cross doesn't mean how the phrase is used in secular life: to endure a thankless task, a difficulty, a strained relationship or a health condition. In Jesus' days the cross had only one outcome: a final, brutal and painful death. Spiritually this still has the meaning for us; our worldly being must die so Jesus can live through me. Paul spoke of this decision in **_Galatians 2:20_** '*I have been crucified with Christ and I no longer live, <u>but Christ lives in me</u>. The life I now live in the body, I live by faith in the Son of God, who loved me and gave Himself for me*'. It is also to assume the cost of following.

To pick up my cross and follow Jesus is tough, death is essential and can be painful, yet the reward is matchless and infinite

---

Jesus never hid the cost of following from His disciples. He stated it plainly (typically in **_Luke: 9, 10_** and **_14_**) and discouraged many who came to Him for the wrong reasons.

With some exceptions our modern-day Gospel has become misleading and un-Biblical. Some outreach programmes even require programme leaders not talk about sin, judgement and hell or the cost of following, so we are bringing in thousands of false converts. How sad! The words of Jesus are proving true even in our 'best' churches.

How few are those with courage to preach what Jesus preached – that following Jesus costs you everything!

To pick up my cross is not to promise to pick up; I can only be a disciple <u>once I already picked up my cross</u>. It isn't a generic cross for everyone. We are each confronted with what we hold dearest and will cost most. Even so, those who really want to follow Christ choose to carry their cross.

Even after I enter by the narrow gate, I continue to deny myself and to carry my cross. There is no slacking off once we find Jesus. The life changes we make before we enter, continue lifelong. If I think I will do what it takes just to be saved and return to my old ways later, then know God is not fooled. He sees our real motivation. The door won't open.

What if it means losing the life you know: home, material prosperity, reputation, job, social standing? What if it means being persecuted or losing actual life or limb? This is what it means in many parts of the world. Or will you be 'pragmatic' and do what the situation requires, yet claim Jesus knows that you love Him and you are just doing what is needed to protect you and your family? Don't be fooled, that isn't to deny yourself but to deny Christ! If we don't love Christ deeply, we will protect our earthly life at the expense of following Jesus.

Have you picked up your cross yet? Are you willing to lose it all, even at church, for being 'too radical' by following as Jesus says?

<u>Follow Jesus</u>

Choosing to follow Jesus needs a human decision: God calls by the Gospel and I make a choice. Even if I am not struck by my sinfulness immediately, I hear God's call. To follow hard after Jesus is an issue of determination and reckless abandon. It is a matter of making a clear choice between two 'Christian' lives:

<u>Option 1</u>: I accommodate Jesus in my life, or

Option 2: I live His life, not mine, as His worker, in His house, His service, His army. Like being in the Armed Forces: ready and in service at all times, with some time to catch up elsewhere! Yet despite this, we don't want it any different.

To follow Jesus is a clear choice: a single life, forever!

The call to follow Jesus is loud and clear and He expects a loud, clear response. Don't ultimately follow for fear of hell or the benefits of heaven. Both will fail. Don't follow for earthly benefits because none are on offer, nor for a fascination with spiritual manifestations. Do it only for who Jesus is and what He did. Only this will last when the trials and the fires come. It is to live flat-out for Jesus, with no life to call 'my own'. God does not begrudge us the pleasures of life - He gave it to us after all. But beware of any pleasure or habit that rules or eats into your time and commitment with Jesus, which occupies your mind and dilutes your focus on your First Love.

We don't appreciate how clear Jesus expects this choice to be. There's no space for anything I love nearly as much as Him. He expects a great distance between Himself and whatever comes next (*'If you don't hate ...'*).

God loves us beyond our dreams. Follow Jesus and He will take care of those you placed a distant second. Let the outcome be what He makes it to be. He will not disappoint you, even if it costs you and others greatly. Jesus promised *'And everyone who has left houses or brothers or sisters or father or mother or wife or children or fields for My sake will receive a hundred times as much and will inherit eternal life'* (**Mat 19:29** and **Mark 10:29**). Do you believe that? May our following cause hardship and pain? Yes. But let it be in God's hands!

Nothing can be better for our loved ones than that they meet Christ. Our example of a living faith in Jesus may be the very witness they need, even if they persecute us in the process. Regardless of what they decide, make your decision clear to yourself and to others, even if it causes friction and separation.

Unless our words and our life's example make our choice clear to our loved ones, they may never find Christ for themselves. Be their living example!

Life with Christ is not a team event. You may be the only one in your religious family to truly follow Jesus. It may pain you greatly, but you may even need to separate from the faith of a deceased loved one who you may now realise never knew Jesus personally. Who do you follow, Jesus or your earthly loved ones?

Beware of the trinkets of this life. Beware the loves, once abandoned, creeping back into your life. **2 Peter 2:22** speaks of a 'true proverb' - *'A dog returns to his vomit.'* Those who don't make a clean break will always return to the old life at some stage. Beware the slow erosion of your clear decision and new loves that begin to compete. Sweep daily, kill weeds quickly. Keep a wide perimeter around your life with Christ like a defensive no-man's land. Don't tolerate a tiny thing, or you may soon find an invasive thorny shrub on your doorstep.

The life in Christ is distant from all else. Unless we enter through the guarded city gates and remain inside, we remain in the valley. True disciples don't just follow in Jesus' general direction and sit on the hill to listen and watch like fans of a celebrity. They are actively involved in intimate closeness, hearing His words and doing as He does and as He commands.

Jesus as 'First Love'

We have referred to Jesus as our First Love on many occasions. It is a variation of the First Commandment of loving God with our heart, soul, mind and strength.

The Father loves the Son and He wants us to adore and love Jesus in the same way. I have found 18 verses in the Gospels that speak of the love between the Father and the Son. Two examples are **John 3:35** *'The Father loves the Son and has placed everything in His hands'* and **Matthew 3:17** *'And a voice from heaven said, "This is My Son, whom I love; with Him I am well pleased"'*. The Father's heart is clear!

As for our First Love for Jesus, we have mentioned these two verses several times before:

Matthew 10:37 *'Anyone who loves his father or mother more than Me is not worthy of Me; anyone who loves his son or daughter more than Me is not worthy of Me'* and

Luke 14:26 *'If anyone comes to Me and does not hate father and mother, wife and children, brothers and sisters--yes, even their own life--such a person cannot be My disciple'*.

We won't discuss Jesus as our First Love any further than these verses because they say it all. Unless our relationship with Jesus is our true 'First Love', there can be no saving relationship. Why would we love Him this much? When we realise our true sinfulness and what Jesus did for us. There is no other way. Can we achieve this on our own? No, but we must choose to love Him as the first choice and priority until He shows us our sinfulness. Our focus is loving commitment: Follow like a true disciple, not like a fan. <u>Choose Him with your time, words, deeds, actions of faith and loving obedience. Choose Him over your earthly first loves when He calls and directs. And He will show Himself to you.</u>

Conclusion

Life outside the gate prepares us for rebirth and for the rest of our lives with Him. The authenticity of our human faith, love, obedience and abandon is being developed and tested.

If we assume salvation happens when we say we believe, then we make surrender and obedience optional. God drives a stake through this! God only gives His Spirit (i.e. rebirth) to those who believe and love, which shows in whether we take Him and His words seriously. While we're outside the gate, He shows us parts of our lives we won't give up on, perhaps due to fear, pride, independence, lack of trust, worldliness and sin.

God decides when our faith, love and commitment to Jesus are true. For some it may take single days, for others many years. Some may even start off in another religion, seeking for the truth. God is merciful. He draws us and encourages us and directs us. He is not in a hurry. He does not prioritise the size but the purity of the Bride. We may go through a lifetime in religion before we come on His terms. Many will never come.

Those who are allowed through the gate will journey on after Jesus. Those who live half-heartedly will assume they are on the narrow road, but actually continue on the broad road. They may look remarkably like true believers but without the Spirit. They are not His, even if so near the gate. They may be fans of Jesus, but not His true followers.

4 Mind Before Heart

'I will give you a new heart and put a new spirit in you; I will remove from you your heart of stone and give you a heart of flesh' (**Eze 36:26**). There is a pre-condition to receiving a new heart: we must change our minds – *metanoia*. We discussed some elements in the previous chapter but this change is much greater than we may think.

It may sound as if finding and following Jesus is an enormous task, but it isn't! The difficulty is what we make of it because of our love for the world and our own independence and even the religious expression we prefer! Instead of losing the earthly life, we want to hang onto it and put the heavenly cloak over it. That is why Jesus warns us so often.

It's God's Grace

We don't search for God; in fact we try to escape from Him. But God, in His great mercy and grace, calls us repeatedly and gives us every opportunity and every reason to believe in Him. God calls us in many different ways, sometimes very obvious ones.

It is easy to glance over the Parables of the Treasure in the Field and the Pearl (**Mat 13:44-45**) and not realise their depth. The treasure in the field was found 'by accident' – the man 'stumbled across' it, i.e. God gave light to someone while they weren't really looking. The merchant, though, was seeking, yet he was probably not expecting such a great value.

Many interpret God's grace as our 'good fortune' that He called and directed us and that we will therefore slip into heaven on His grace. No, once we find a treasure we can inspect it and get to know it well but it doesn't make it ours. We can't grab it or claim it as if it is a right. We must accept the full cost, as both men in the Parables had to do – they sold everything. This aspect is often overlooked in Christianity.

Finding the treasure only shows us the great gift of Christ, but it cannot be ours without the cost!

What is our task? Before we receive a new heart we must change our minds. At the raw heart level we need Jesus to save us and we cannot be saved unless we have new priorities. Cheap salvation is no salvation.

Everything Must Go

Abandoning my life to Jesus seldom happens in an instant because there is the core of our being to let go of.

Jesus And Our Treasures

Our struggle to receive Jesus' gift is a direct inverse of our easy, nice lives. In **_Luke 16:19-31_** (the Rich Man and Lazarus) Abraham said to the Rich Man: *'Remember that in your lifetime you received your good things, while Lazarus received bad things.'* We cling to our kingdom of 'good things' too: money, pride, attachment and achievements, popularity, physical appearance, self-obsession and independence from God. We will only give it up if we find something more valuable.

Human beings think a good earthly life is to our benefit but it seriously limits our choice for Jesus. There is only space for one treasure. The more we love our lives, the less the chance we will let go. We must empty our hands to receive God's gift. In reality we should ask God to help us put things in their proper place and get rid of everything that can distract us because it can seduce us into hell! Worldly possessions are <u>not</u> the sign that God is pleased with us!

<u>The poor</u> (not just in money) <u>have a distinct advantage over the rich for salvation</u> (*'Truly I tell you, it is hard for someone who is rich to enter the kingdom of heaven. Again I tell you, it is easier for a camel to go through the eye of a needle than for someone who is rich to enter the kingdom of God'* **Mat 19:23-24**). What about other treasures such as our position, our pride, accolades of others for our goodness and charity, etc? In **Luke 16:15** Jesus warns *'What people value highly is detestable in God's sight.'* Our worldly loves make us very unwilling to give it all up for Jesus (*'Dear children, keep yourselves from idols'* **1 John 5:21**).

Note also that it is not only about <u>having</u> earthly riches; we are also bound by what we desire, even if we don't yet have it or have little. The Parable of the Sower says <u>*'the deceitfulness of wealth and the desires for other things'*</u> will stifle and kill the faith of many before it reaches maturity (**Mark 4:19**).

On some levels there is little difference in attachment between the Haves and Have Nots: some already have the riches they are attached to; others still desire them, but they are as attached!

God knows what captivates our hearts and He will challenge us with the things we love more than Jesus. He will confront us with our treasure piece by piece until we give up the world at our core. It is as if He holds up treasures asking 'Do you love Me enough to give this up for Me?' After that we must figuratively (sometimes even literally?) put it in the fire ourselves. He will not wrench it from our hands; we must bring it. This makes it so painful. This takes every effort! Can we be attached and go to heaven? No. The rich young ruler was obedient in all else but couldn't let go of His riches and he went away sad. His stuff was his god.

To lose something by an accident does not mean we are no longer attached to it. Putting it in the fire is the act of losing it in our hearts. It can be gut-wrenching because we are so aware. Sometimes we may need a few attempts before we really let go.

The journey of discipleship ahead is tough and we will not last the distance if we don't burn our bridges and our treasures. Otherwise we will be like the Israelites who longed back to the deadly comforts of Egypt at every difficult turn.

I remember so well how God placed me before a great earthly love, a considerable investment in time and money and very dear hobby and lifestyle of mine. I came to realise it was too important in my life and might stand in the way of forsaking all for Jesus and could limit my ministry in His service. It is not sinful but it is something that could hinder ('... *let us throw off everything that hinders...*' **Heb 12:1**).

I handed it over to God and asked Him to remove it if it would cause my relationship with Him or His work through me or His name to suffer in the future. In this case God gave it back to me even though I was ready to part with it. I did stray on it once more but now I keep a very watchful eye on it, not to invest precious time and money into it. I just enjoy it for what it is, as and when. I know it has the potential to rear its head again and become a consuming treasure. I remain committed to letting it go, so I guard my mind closely. God is not against us enjoying things, but they cannot stand in His way.

Once we abandon our lives to Jesus the battle is won. Whether a much loved or a little loved part of my life, the answer remains the same – 'Lord, all is Yours, for the sake of knowing Christ Jesus'. I cannot do this successfully in self-martyrdom because my true heart will return at an unguarded moment. But when Jesus becomes my treasure of great value, giving up becomes a joy.

Paul says *'What is more, I consider everything a <u>loss</u> because of the surpassing worth of knowing Christ Jesus my Lord, for whose sake I have lost all things. I consider them garbage, that I may gain Christ'* (**Phil 3:8**). The Greek word translated as 'loss' also means a 'bad deal' that results in a penalty or forfeiture. Paul speaks of the things that were lost as 'garbage'. This is in the same spirit as *'if you don't <u>hate</u> your father or mother ... even your own life'* – the distance is so great when we find Jesus that our old life becomes 'garbage' against *'the surpassing worth of knowing Christ'*.

Some will go so far but they will not sacrifice everything. God will not accept even a single thing that remains too important to me, sinful or not, because it shows I hadn't surrendered to Jesus. If I rule out submitting anything, then by default I rule out Jesus.

There is something that often remains unspoken in the modern church: If I place <u>any human relationship</u> higher than Jesus, God will not accept my 99.9% surrender. Everything must be set under His Son's Lordship. If there is <u>any sinful relationship</u> or cherished sinful memory in my life that I refuse to break from permanently, then God is not in that faith, regardless of what churches teach or remain silent on. Society and even a church may accept that relationship, but God alone decides who shares in His kingdom. This goes even further and extends to those who defend or approve a sinful behaviour of others (*'Although they know God's righteous decree that those *who do such things deserve death, they not only continue to do these very things but also approve of those who practice them'* **Rom 1:32**). Before God's definition there aren't 'lovely Christian people' who live in sinful relationships or defends them, even if the world accepts or applauds them.

For the avoidance of doubt then, can I decide not to surrender all and be saved, but just won't be a part of His 'inner circle' of disciples? No! Can I be saved and agree to give up something in the future (e.g. a sinful relationship)? No. Why? Because He is choosing a Bride for Christ and won't allow people in who choose the sinful or the worldly over His Son. Many may give up partially, but they will remain outside.

Why is this important? Because Jesus makes it clear these are not God's preferences but His preconditions for being in His family (i.e. salvation).

It is false to teach that we can believe, love and surrender partially and be saved!

The broad road leads right up to the narrow gate. We can get so near but still outside. God doesn't reward being close. We can be around church our entire lives and love the way we love God and church, and still end up in hell.

One day you may be reminded of a time when Jesus called you to follow Him. '*"Come now, let us settle the matter," says the LORD ...*' (**Is 1:18**). Perhaps you are refusing to let go of some of earthly loves or sinful behaviours. What does it in effect mean? That God calls and you won't respond; the world, the flesh and the devil call and you do.

Mind Change v Heart Change

There are two deadly versions of Christianity:

Condition 1: People call themselves Christian and even born-again but there is no true commitment to Jesus and His words. Their fruit can only be bad because nothing changed: they prayed a prayer but remain far off, even if they are firmly in the church. This is certain spiritual death.

Condition 2: This is more difficult to spot: they have been struck by Jesus. They decided to change their lives, obey and follow Him. They dealt with immediate sins but they do not break with the remaining ones. This is the defeated Christian life without the Spirit. They partially changed their mind but haven't received a new heart yet. Paul writes *'Therefore, there is now no condemnation for those who are in Christ Jesus, because through Christ Jesus the law of the Spirit who gives life has set you free from the law of sin and death'* (**Rom 8:1-2**). This triumph is not yet true for them.

Many sincere, hardworking believers live in this second state and are active in the church. They decided to follow Jesus so there is no longer the fun of blatant sin, but there is also no joy and peace in Christ. This is the graveyard of the Many. It is a difficult place. The result? Moments of joy followed by misery, doubt, self-righteousness and/or judgmentalism. The life of highs and lows of the unredeemed Christian.

This is a life of poverty: 'Distinctly Christian', but not overcomers. Good Christians, but not filled with the Spirit. Knowledge of Jesus, but no intimacy. Backbone of the local church, but not a reborn child of God. 'Almost There', but still on the broad road, needing rebirth by the Spirit of Christ.

Sadly, both of these states are common-place religion. Their own version of faith rules their lives where Jesus is an add-on and where they give up what doesn't cost too much. It's a life of works, even if they strongly oppose any notion of works. It is life in the departure lounge. They increase in knowledge but their faith does not grow because there isn't the final abandon. It is of them that Paul said to Timothy *'having a form of godliness but denying its power'* (**_2 Timothy 3:5_**).

It is easier to be a principled follower than a Spirit-altered Christ disciple

---

It can be disconcerting to accept that, even if I have modified my behaviour a great deal, I am not saved. Even if we were to physically remove an eye, it does not change the lustful heart. Removing an eye merely puts seeing beyond our reach. We must still break from our sin in our hearts.

Without Christ there is no difference between earthly 'holy' (i.e. good behaviour) and 'unholy' (bad behaviour). Both are Christ-less and Spirit-less

---

Without deep love and passionate affection for Jesus there is neither favour from God, nor an authentic witness to the world. Unless there is a complete change of mind, God will never grant a complete change of heart.

The Chasm

In the account of the Rich Man and Lazarus (**_Luke 16:19-31_**) the rich man asked Abraham to send over Lazarus to dip his finger into the water to wet his tongue because of his thirst. Abraham replied that there is a chasm between heaven and hell so no-one can go between them (**_v26_**). That chasm is permanent. Once in hell there is no access to heaven, and there will be no comfort from those in heaven to those in hell either.

After this life our eternity is fixed. No second chances, no Purgatory, no reincarnations, no prayers of the living

---

There is also a chasm on the earth and it is sited between where I am outside the gate, and the small gate itself. To cross it I must have a new heart. For that I must change my mind. If I don't, then that chasm will become permanent in hell.

We find it easy to point fingers at the obvious failings of the wayward: the drunks, the addicts and the vile. Their problem is easy to spot, even to themselves. Their obvious failings make their chasm wide but it can be shallow: there may be many failings but they are very aware. Their chasm can fill in quickly once they see the light of Christ, because deep down they know they are a sinful mess. And it will be clear for anyone to distinguish between their old life and the new because the change is so dramatic.

It is more difficult to spot the hidden things in our own Christian lives. Like the Pharisee I can be so convinced of my own 'goodness', yet my self-righteousness is a deep chasm that keeps me from salvation.

Beware of the place so near to the gate for a long time. Perhaps we laid down many things already, so the chasm is very narrow. We feel content with our righteousness and our professed faith. Yet God pointed out a specific issue to us so many times and we refuse. We think we are saved and that it is a matter of choice whether we deal with it or not. Yet it makes that chasm very deep – we have no intention of giving it up. The more we refuse, the harder the heart and the deeper the chasm. We refuse because it defines us. This is the 'your life' Jesus says we are to hate, in comparison. To everyone from the outside we may appear so good and holy, yet God knows the one attachment that keeps us away from Him.

People with many burdens may soon lay them all down and enter. I, on the other hand, in my self-righteousness and my assumed salvation, will remain outside the gate with my 'acceptable' or hidden sin. I 'gave my heart to Jesus', even as a young child, lived a 'good Christian life' so I may think I am saved, yet God disagrees. And there, outside the gate, I may stay into all eternity. This one thing will be the death of me.

For you this one issue may be something that you consider of little consequence, like gossiping or racism (which is hatred and pride), perhaps unforgiveness or that one relationship you won't give up, that one attachment, or unforgiveness, anger, envy, covetousness, greed or that secret sinful memory you cherish. Perhaps it is one thing you did that you refuse to ask forgiveness from the person you harmed. Your pride will not allow you. You will rather die than give up your 'one thing'. Yes, that chasm is not wide, but it is deep. It has deepened over the years because you hardened your heart time and again. Beware, God may soon confirm your decision and harden your heart for you as He did with Pharaoh.

God does not count the many things we give up, but a single issue: who is lord: me or Jesus? He isn't interested in percentages. He measures 100% or nothing. It is ON / OFF; either in one position or the other. Anything less than 100% abandon and the switch is OFF – we have not given up our lordship and we only allow God in the confines we stipulate. Our one treasure is still greater than Jesus. Our 99% does not show our great meritorious effort; instead our 1% refusal shows our stubborn, deadly self-righteous flaw for refusing to yield to Christ. The Lord and Saviour are inseparably One. We don't get the one without the other.

If you realise you are still outside the gate, are you prepared to ask God to reveal, even very publicly, what holds you back? Do you realise that it is better to lose all your pride than go to hell with your pride intact? *'If your eye causes you to sin, pluck it out ...'* (**Mark 9:47**).

Others look up to us and we be comfortable in our own goodness. To the outside world we are indistinguishable from narrow road believers. We may even die for the cause of Christ because we look so alike. **1 Corinthians 13** is our reality - even if I give up my body to be burnt or give up everything I have, and I don't have *agape* love, I gain nothing. God knows I am spiritually dead. I must change my mind in the clearest decision before my heart can follow!

It's a 'First Love' Relationship

The true life with Christ is like a human love relationship: it starts in a meeting and ends in a wedding in heaven. How does a good human relationship progress towards marriage? Not on a fixed timeline; some get there quicker than others. It progresses based on growing mutual knowledge and love. There is a meeting, an agreement to see one another again and finding out more about one another. It progresses to 'going out' – a more serious relationship, then engagement with the gift of a ring and finally marriage on the wedding day. Hardly ever is there an engagement at the first meeting!

In a love relationship a couple act like loved ones before the engagement, not only after the engagement. All the basics are in place. Engagement links the two people in an official declaration of love, exclusive relationship and a promise to marry.

After the engagement the love and the relationship will deepen. The future bride and groom do things together and begin to plan for their wedding day and married life when there is no more separation. The life before the wedding has the same love nature as the life after the wedding.

Our saving, loving relationship with Jesus is similar, but far more profound. The meeting is hearing the Gospel, then a time of finding out more, then our decision to become more serious with Jesus as a first choice, followed by engagement (salvation), our journey together on the earth, and finally the wedding in heaven. One thing is certain: there is hardly ever an 'engagement' (rebirth) on Day 1! Sadly, as with human relationships, many fall by the wayside at each stage. The same is true with our relationship with Jesus. God never falls away, but we do.

God accepts only our First Love relationship with Jesus. We must forsake all competing loves. He is patient but finally only one outcome satisfies Him.

Seek First the Kingdom of God

Is Jesus my deepest love and desire? He either is or He isn't. What is the evidence? According to God it's loving obedience!

The Pharisee asked Jesus *'Teacher, what must I do to inherit the kingdom?'* Jesus did not give him a method but gave hm the Greatest Commandment *'You shall love the Lord your God with all your heart, with all your soul, with all your mind and with all your strength'* (**Mat 22:37**).

Outside the gate is where our earthly loved ones will learn we have a new First Priority. There is bound to be separation with old shared values and priorities. We soon find out what Jesus meant with the cost of following. Others, even professing Christians, dislike the impact our new priority has on their own plans and their plans for your life. Parents want children to be successful and 'use their education'. Children may hear 'you are throwing your life away' and 'we sacrificed our lives to give you every opportunity'. 'We have always been a good God-fearing family, why are you doing this?' With adult water baptism, religious families may say 'You are bringing shame on our family name.' Single people hear they will never be married if they live this kind of life. Younger parents hear they must be career-minded for their children's better future. Older ones hear 'protect your retirement', or 'guard your children's inheritance' or 'don't abandon grandchildren' when serving God, etc, etc. These are very real issues.

The impact of obedience goes even further: loved ones, often very religious churchgoers, may become active enemies and persecute you on your path with Jesus (**Mat 10:36**) because you no longer share their passions and beliefs. [A note of caution: ensure their opposition is because of our love and obedience to Christ, not our objectionable behaviour!]

How must we respond to them? In the same way Jesus expects us to respond to all 'enemies': love them and pray for them (**Mat 5:43-48**). Show them the love of Christ by loving them, while standing unwaveringly with Jesus and His words. Go the extra mile – treat them with even greater love, doing more than what can be expected (*'But I tell you not to resist an evil person. If someone slaps you on your right cheek, turn to him the other also; if someone wants to sue you and take your tunic, let him have your cloak as well; and if someone forces you to go one mile, go with him two'* **Mat 5:39-41**).

The modern church abandoned the simple truth of following Jesus: to follow His pattern of life. Sadly someone can be an exemplary Christian, a successful pastor or speaker, yet without lives that resemble Christ's. We must seek His kingdom and righteousness first.

I Am The LORD!

Jesus did not die so that only a select few can enter heaven. **John 3:16** says *'so that <u>whoever</u> believes in Him shall not perish but have eternal life'*. Whoever. That means anyone. *'My Father's house has many rooms; if that were not so, would I have told you that I am going there to prepare a place for you?'* (**John 14:2**). He invites everyone.

God does not restrict numbers but quality. He does not want any to be lost (**2 Pet 3:9**) but heaven to be filled to the brim with every person who ever lived. Yet 'Only a Few' choose Him over all else. In the parable of the wedding feast many were invited, but they chose to live for their own priorities and lives over coming to the feast of God. God only chooses those who choose Jesus. *'I am the Lord: that is My name! I will not yield My glory to another or My praise to idols'* (**Is 42:8**). Jesus is Lord. He will not be diminished or share His Lordship!

What will the wedding feast be? *'No eye has seen, no ear has heard, and no mind has imagined what God has prepared for those who love Him'* (**1 Cor 2:9** NLT). It will be an eternity of unimaginable bliss and joy.

Many think to follow Jesus is a burden. He interferes with their earthly life – can't do this, give time to that, give money to the next. Yet Jesus doesn't tell us to give up anything. We can keep every little thing we want and even get more: bigger houses, bigger cars, more stuff and a greater earthly life. Yet if we want Him, He stands at the narrow gate. It is like a security turnstile gate in a security fence: enter on invitation only, one at a time, no baggage (only a cross!) There are no other alternatives available. God guards the Gate (the Bride of Christ) jealously. We can choose to stay where we are or we can go to Him with empty hands.

Earthly dreams, desires, sins and possessions are heavy, oppressive loads. But once we hand it over to Him, His load is light because we only carry what He gives us.

By now you may realise why Jesus says so few in our churches are truly His. Many believe they are following Him, but so few people change their minds to give up and choose Jesus as their greatest prize.

The Great Value of a Free Gift

Much is made in the church of the free gift of salvation. Yet there is a grave under-assessment of this truth. The gift is very valuable on four levels:

- Firstly, the high cost to God who provided the gift. The cost is much greater than we can imagine and we hardly ever meditate on this under the Spirit, so we won't grasp God's insistence that we love Jesus most, and why He will not share His Son with those who don't want Him alone.
- Secondly, the gift of salvation sets us free from an eternal punishment far worse than we can fathom.
- Thirdly, the free gift has much greater benefits than we understand: being a part of the family of God, the heavenly life and that it really is eternal.
- Lastly, to receive the gift needs empty hands. We only realise why when we understand the first three points.

Our carnal minds really don't think this is worth much, which is why we simply cannot see past our earthly desires and keep demanding health, wealth and happiness. When we are reborn we receive a glimpse, a deposit, of the joy and peace of oneness with God.

God promises the only Fine Gift worth having to those who come on His terms: Himself. His promises include:

- oneness with Christ (***John 17:23***),
- never to leave or forsake us (***Deut 31:6*** and ***Heb 13:5***),
- always be with us, even to the end of the age (***Mat 28:20),***
- His peace, but not as the world gives peace (***John 14:27***),
- to provide all we need spiritually, so that our joy may be complete (***John 15:11***),
- the fruit of the Spirit (***Gal 5:22-23***) and
- provision for our daily needs (***Mat 6:25-34***).

His earthly provision for us is enough – His daily bread. It may be meagre pickings at times but He satisfies us with a new vision where even this is a feast at His table. Our experience of these small mercies may be so rich that it can at times drive us to actual tears of gratitude.

It Takes Faith!

The worldly life and the faith life in Christ are polar opposites. To follow Jesus the way He says means the end of life as we know it. We don't easily give up the life we know for what we cannot see. It needs faith to depend on God to provide for us rather than look to our own strength. It takes faith to abandon this life and be convinced that there really is an eternal life to come. But we must step out in faith.

Most professing believers live a hybrid life of good morals, partial faith and trying to buy insurance for heaven, yet they live a life of the earth. This is life enhancement and behaviour change, not a changed mind.

This is the life of the Christian Atheist; Christian by name, atheist by nature!

Ask yourself: If someone you love made a real mess of their life and gave you full control to help them sort it out, would you make their lives good or miserable, the best or the worst? Of course we would seek their best! It may require tough decisions but it will always be for their long-term best.

Jesus wants us to understand the Father's heart *'If you, then, though you are evil, know how to give good gifts to your children, how much more will your Father in heaven give good gifts to those who ask Him!'* (**Mat 7:11**) He is infinitely more dependable than the best parent. But it takes resolute faith to believe that!

We cannot receive God's best unless trust God and give Him complete control

'And without faith it is impossible to please God, because anyone who comes to Him must believe that He exists and that He rewards those who earnestly seek Him' (**Heb 11:6**).

My Own Decision

Against this background, what was my personal decision?

I resolved before my Father in heaven that, with the Spirit, I will spend the rest of my days to worship, love, obey and follow Jesus, regardless of cost. As the song goes '<u>I have decided to follow Jesus, no turning back, no turning back</u>'!

I realised there were many parts of my life that did not reflect Christ in me. I started intentionally obeying every teaching of Jesus I could find. Some came with more difficulty; with others I am still battling. But this I can say for sure: My mind is changed! Forever! With God's grace I made a ruthless commitment to obey everything because Jesus is above all else.

My mind is made up. By His grace is my direction fixed and irrevocable

My Faith Challenge

Throughout my faith life I lived in the error of the worldly church: I am saved when I say I believe. However, God showed me only the faith that He validates with rebirth by the Spirit is His salvation. Everything else is false.

My greatest faith challenge was to believe God for the true rebirth of the Spirit, especially when God waited so long to open the door for me. His Spirit is the only true proof of the existence of God, of authenticity of faith and of salvation.

Living out the worldly church's deficient message was easy. It costs little and it delivers instant results! Yet when God showed me the truth, and when I saw so little evidence of the true Spirit life in the vast majority, even leaders, in the church, how could I be sure the definite article of the Spirit was possible for me? Surely I should see the evidence of many Spirit-filled people. Yet, based on God's truth, many churches may not even have one true saint!

It is hard to over-emphasise how difficult this was. How does one believe that only the definite rebirth by the Spirit is the God's way when it goes against all that is taught and written? It even contrasts the teachings of some of the finest Bible expositors. How does one believe that the journey to find Jesus may take a lifetime, even for the true seeker, when churches teach it is an instant thing when you pray in a sincere moment? How does one believe this when leaders of large growing churches don't have this insight into the salvation they are preaching?

This was my faith challenge: to believe against the worldly church evidence that there is more to salvation than what is taught across the theological spectrum.

Do you have any idea how self-doubt sets in when God chooses to show you a truth in Scripture, that in retrospect is so self-evident, but that you missed because you were blinded by the preconceived ideas of the earthly church, and this truth contradicts the faith of so many 'godly believers'? And then to share this truth? Yet God brought my doubts back in line repeatedly: 'Which of these things have I not said?'

How I praise the Almighty God that He can be trusted! He reveals Himself to the little ones who truly seek Him, however long it takes, even against all the evidence in the worldly church and against the words of many wise and learned! It does indeed take every effort to find Him!

Concluding Remarks

To the dismay of many, I fear, the evidence of Scripture is that for the vast majority the narrow gate to salvation is much further down the faith path than they assume. And the gate is much smaller than we are led to believe.

God gives us such clarity in Scripture, if only we will listen. Study the Words of God and determine the truth for yourself

---

5 Seeking to Find Jesus

Introduction

I cannot stress enough that each of us is responsible for what we believe and for seeking Jesus for ourselves. We are active participants in our own faith. <u>No-one else can find Jesus for us</u>. We must *'Make every effort to enter by the narrow gate'* (**Luke 13:24**).

God's truth is in His Word. He guides us by His Spirit. It is dangerous to depend on others to feed us. They are signposts to truths but we must confirm their words in Scripture. If you are serious about finding Jesus, then go look for Him! *'You have one Teacher'* (**Mat 23:8**), whatever your favourite teacher says. If you cannot yet attest to the Spirit's rebirth in your life, then study this chapter carefully. The key to finding Jesus may well lie in seeking Jesus in the manner He is to be found. Study the Bible deliberately, daily.

It is up to you, under the Spirit, to seek out the Truth

Love the One God Loves Most!

There is a story, and a film (*The Longest Ride*) with a similar story line, of someone of great wealth, with a much loved one who died (in the story it is the father's son and in the film the man's wife). At the man's death an auction was held of the vast number of paintings of exceptional value of the masters they collected together. The first item on auction was an amateur painting of the man's loved one. It had no commercial value. Only one person showed any interest – someone who knew the man intimately and who knew of his great love for his loved one. At that point the auction was stopped and the rest of the man's will was read out: whoever bought this painting would also receive the vast fortune of all the rest of the paintings.

The reason became obvious: <u>whoever recognised the loved one as the real treasure of the rich man, would receive the gift of all the other treasures that belonged to him too</u>.

This is just a story but it explains much about salvation and the Gospel.

Why does the Father love Jesus so much? Because *'God is love'* (***1 John 4:8***). The purest and highest love exists within the Godhead. And because Jesus left His heavenly throne to die for the people He created, in the greatest act of loving obedience to the Father. The Father wants us to worship, love and celebrate His Son for who He is and what He did.

Hollywood is keen to depict Jesus as a handsome man, often with long flowing hair. This is not the image from Scripture. ***Isaiah 53:2*** says *'He had no beauty or majesty to attract us to Him, nothing in His appearance that we should desire Him.'* God wants us to love His Son for no other reason than for who He is and what He has done; not for His appearance, nor for earthly blessings or heavenly promises.

The path to the Father will be much clearer when we understand what He wants from us. As in the film, the Father says in effect 'All My love and blessings are yours, but you must love My Son above all else'. The Father adores Him (*'This is My Son, whom I love; with Him I am well pleased'* ***Mat 3:17***). The Father saves only on this basis. We can't just acknowledge Jesus and have warm affection towards Him.

God is gathering a Bride as a love gift for His Son. If we want heaven then we must love the One He loves most: His Son, Jesus Christ

Know the Cost

We return to the cost of following Jesus. To seek and find Jesus means to lose our religion, i.e. what we think saving faith is and how we choose to exercise our Christian faith. However deeply we hold our convictions and however sincerely we practice our faith, any self-styled religion must die. Instead we must believe God's truth and live by His words alone.

We must lose our primary affiliation to any group or set of beliefs, and attach ourselves only to Jesus

In the same way that people from other faiths must lose their much-loved religion to find Christ, so Christians must lose their unbiblical religion too! To have Christ we must believe and live out what is true. There is only space for Christ, not for the religion of Christianity, however convinced you may be that your brand of the faith is correct!

It is the most painful and disconcerting thing to be untied from our religion. We must let go of our <u>first love</u> for what we find so comfortable and the people we share it with: a sense of closeness life experiences, and emotions tied to our religion. Following Jesus may bring division even in the earthly church family.

During His time on the earth Jesus did not side with His earthly family first but He gave priority to His *'brothers and sisters and mother*' in faith. Jesus could bring us before the same choice! He did not bring peace as the world understands, but the sword. It divides between God and the world. There is no place in His kingdom for those who do not stand up for Him (***Mat 10:33***). Our light must shine before the world.

We must take these warnings seriously. This cost is real.

'Seeking Jesus' In Perspective

When people are first reached with the Gospel they may become aware they are lost. Yet most professing Christians find it is difficult to imagine they can still be lost. Once they are a part of the 'church family', especially many years at the core of church life, they think it's impossible that they can still be lost, especially when they are amongst others who think the same. They were told or assumed they are saved and many cannot be persuaded otherwise.

The single most deadly condition in the modern church is 'perpetual lostness': one generation evangelises the next into their own lostness

---

Everyone believes they must be right because the organised church tells them they are; yet, according to Jesus, most in the earthly church are lost themselves!

As generations roll on the heavenly church remains where it has been since the book of Acts – in Jesus. Yet the earthly church moves ever further from Jesus and ever closer to the world – a logical progression when most in the church are still of the world. More worrying is that the church is not aware of the deadly condition. Mention the possibility and people think others is lost but not they. How will the earthly church be confronted if so many <u>are</u> the condition?

Those who the Spirit wakes up must be honest about their state to have any hope of finding Christ. Paul encourages: *'Examine yourselves to see whether you are in the faith; test yourselves. Do you not realise that Christ Jesus is in you—unless, of course, you fail the test? And I trust that you will discover that we have not failed the test'* (**2 Cor 13:5-6**).

Ultimately this is the test: did you receive the Spirit as a definite experience and do you have the ongoing testimony of the Spirit to your spirit that you are saved? How will it show in your day-to-day life? Not in church activities, but in oneness with Jesus (*'Remain in Me, as I also remain in you'* **John 15:4**), in loving one another (*'By this everyone will know that you are My disciples, if you love one another'* **John 13:35**) and in obedience to what He commanded (*'For whoever does the will of My Father in heaven is My brother and sister and mother'* **Mat 12:50**, **Mark 3:35**, **Luke 8:21**)

God promises that if we seek with all our heart, we will find (**Jer 29:13**). But when we seek Jesus, nothing can be off-limits and we cannot come with preconditions.

We don't approach Jesus to negotiate eternal life; we submit to Him in complete surrender

---

C. S. Lewis said, *'We don't come to Him as bad people trying to become good people; we come as rebels to lay down our arms.'* We don't come to change a little, but to be transformed. We obey Jesus' teachings but not to obtain the heavenly prize, like a payment for being good. Let heaven be a secondary issue, but let us seek to *'know Christ and Him crucified'* (**1 Cor 2:2**).

In evangelism our task is to make disciples and teach them to obey Jesus' words (**Mat 28:19-20**). We can encourage them to follow, but only God saves. He won't do it any quicker because we push people before their hearts are abandoned.

Making disciples is more than declaring the Gospel. It is to teach others the full truth of Jesus. Our task is to lead them on their journey, not to convince them to say 'yes'.

We must get over the idea that Jesus will bend His own words to win people over. He is the Sovereign Lord and He isn't waiting with cupped hands, begging to enter our lives. Nothing could be further from the Sovereign God!

Seeking and Salvation

We already discussed the assumption that we are saved when we decide to follow Jesus. After that people assume there are different options of how to live the Christian life (since we are already 'saved', these are assumed optional):

- as a carnal Christian (claiming salvation but continuing in worldliness and independence), or
- being actively involved in spiritual and other activities of the church, or
- to be radical and make serious life changes for Jesus (living near to God, being led by His Spirit, etc).

Scripture only affirms one type of following: radically altered children of God. Jesus does not have tag-along disciples, even serious and sincere. I don't get saved yet remain a disobedient rebel and decide later whether to ditch the rebellion. God accepts only those who have left their rebellion.

Jesus repeatedly warns us out of love and concern because He alone knows the enormity of eternity without Him. He gives us every opportunity; He pursues us in love so we will not go lost. We must find Him, or He says in effect 'don't bother!'

My Path to Finding Jesus

<u>This was my journey</u>: In anyone's books I was a believer: Bible knowledge, speaking, praying, leadership and more. I finally stopped pressing my 'override button' every time I had doubts and really started seeking Jesus intensely.

Measured by the words of Jesus my faith didn't stack up. I realised with a great shock I'd fooled myself for too long and that my starting point was wrong. I'd progressed spiritually during those years and I was active in the church but I was never reborn. The change I needed comes only as a gift from God. He gave me a discontent with my deficient faith but I still had to seek to find Him. Was I saved? No.

Most of my life I lived a fairly restrained 'Christian' life. There were few 'gross sins', so I fell into the typical 'ethical life' trap – self-righteousness! I couldn't grasp my own sinfulness. I finally asked Jesus to show me my life as He sees it. Suddenly deeper things poured out: prejudices, aspirations, selfish ambitions, fears, anger and the like. I realised I was not sinful because I sinned, but because my nature is sinful, so even my very best thoughts and actions are sinful.

I began taking Jesus' words seriously. I realised my thoughts were wrong long before my actions – just what Jesus said! I also still worried what would happen if I really let God control my life.

By now I'd already followed Jesus for many years and had been used in a number of demonstrable ways. Yet there were things I hadn't realised I had to let go of. Jesus was important to me, but He wasn't Number One.

I would like to address an important matter before we go on: During my life as a professing Christian I glossed over passages about having to love Jesus above all else. Yet, I <u>never</u> heard in <u>any</u> church that if I don't love Jesus more than anything else, I am not worthy of Him. Not once! But this is what Jesus said! Nor was there a single sermon on the critical importance of obedience in <u>all</u> my years in the church either.

No-one <u>ever</u> said that not giving up everything is an issue of salvation. No-one said if we don't forgive others, we cannot be forgiven ourselves – yet Jesus says so. Or not dying to anger, lies, lust and jealousy means there is no place in God's kingdom for us. Yet Jesus says so! No-one said when we start this walk, we leave our old life behind for good, seriously, and if we don't, we cannot be His. Yet Jesus says so! No-one told me that my actions show whether my faith in God is true. Of course the Bible says so, BUT THE CHURCH DOESN'T! There isn't salvation because 'I believe in Jesus'. Or space for unbroken sin and wilful disobedience!

I am not shifting the blame at all. I am responsible! However, the church's silence on the clear words of Scripture meant I didn't take those words seriously either. I am just astounded that the earthly organisation that professes Jesus' divinity and salvation will choose to elevate some passages while it ignores the clear words in the rest of Scripture. They aren't difficult to find or understand; we just ignore them!

I did all the believing and claiming salvation through grace by grabbing hold of it, confessing positively and assuming my identity in Christ. Nothing changed. Why? Because that is not God's way of salvation!

My point is that the church should be leading us in the truth, and in most churches this just does not happen! Why is this? Because in the main the wider church hardly represents the full truth of God, in all likelihood because so many leaders *themselves are not saved according to the words of Jesus. Instead of standing for the words of Christ, many say that to do what He commands is salvation by works. It shows the state of their own hearts.*

This showed me <u>I remain primarily responsible for the truth of what I believe</u>. <u>I am responsible for studying the Word myself</u> and asking God to reveal His will and His truths to me. <u>I remain responsible for seeking and finding Jesus</u> for myself. Never apart from the mercy and grace of God, but I must seek Him for myself. And so must every other person. We must take every verse of Scripture seriously. <u>We ignore this responsibility at our own eternal peril!</u>

Even in the midst of seeking Jesus, I was often going backwards on important matters, and my prayer life suffered. It was a deep struggle.

Then the light came on. God showed me I cannot find Him on my own. <u>If I want to please Jesus I have to ask Him to tell me what He wants and to help me overcome!</u> He wants to help. Once I started leaning on Jesus, I was able to let go of the things I clung onto and He showed me other things He hated.

The biggest insight was when God showed me I was not making progress because my 'central motivation' was wrong: Jesus wasn't the object of my adoration. The church's message is only to 'believe in Jesus' so it never occurred to me that God insists on a 'First Love' relationship.

I was cleaning up my life in my own way to stay out of hell and to go to heaven. I'd made Jesus into a vehicle for getting what I wanted

---

I soon realised I could not 'work up' enough love for Jesus to satisfy the Father. Sometimes in human love two people can get on exceptionally well as friends but no more. Then, on a day, something happens and everything changes. Perhaps a character trait in the other person comes to the fore, or they show a selfless side that the other person never saw before. All of a sudden there is a new, meaningful reality that puts the person in a whole new light and it becomes the foundation for moving from friendship to love.

With Jesus the foundation for moving from friendship (*phileo* love) to deep love (*agape* love) is when God gifts us Godly sorrow for our sins and we realise that the sinless, perfect Jesus paid for our personal sins. At that point there is a reason for a deep love relationship.

The turning point for me came one day when I watched *The Passion of the Christ*, the film on the final days of Jesus. My heart broke when I saw the very graphic scene where Jesus was strapped to a post with bare back, His body literally being ripped to shreds. For the first time God opened my eyes to the suffering of Jesus. He endured it for my sins, even for the sins I committed that same day. It drove me to tears. Godly sorrow! Another was when God gave me the greatest fear for Him over sins I committed casually. It was truly frightening. (I still have a picture I took on the day to remind me of my sinfulness and Jesus' death for me.)

Although these were such deep experiences, I was still not changed at my core. Unless I was sorry enough to stop, cast myself on Jesus, choose Him over everything and wave goodbye to my earthly life, all my tears were meaningless. Being tearful and fearful without a real change makes no difference. Was I saved? No. It was only a start.

Choosing Jesus over all else must be fixed and permanent. Bridges must be burnt, with every intention never to return!

To look back means I am unfit for the kingdom (**Luke 9:62**). Yet it can be a slow, agonising process as we are being cut free.

Putting Jesus first meant being confronted with my higher loves. I had to realise that this new life would bring division. God placed many agonising relationships before me in my mind's eye. Even if I didn't have to part with them then, I already had to place them a distant second, one after the other. That didn't mean I loved Jesus with all my heart, soul, mind and strength as a 'heart feeling'. But this was what I had to do: to choose Jesus as my highest commitment and first preference and show it in my daily practical choices.

I stopped fooling myself and acknowledged openly and regularly before God that I was lost, even after following Jesus for so many years. My prayers changed instantly. I no longer had the long list of requests; instead I asked God to show me Jesus. And I asked Him to help me love Jesus as much as He wanted me to love Him because I couldn't do it myself. Jesus could not become my *First Lo*ve unless God changed me. I developed an even stronger faith in Jesus, but was I saved? No. Why not? Because I had still not received the Spirit.

I realised I needed to be reborn of God!

I started doing what Jesus commanded; not to earn my salvation, but because Jesus is my chosen LORD. I spent daily time with Him, deliberately, to get close to Him. I was serious about finding Him. In several of my prayers I said 'Lord, I am not going anywhere until You bless me, even if I die while I seek!' This isn't salvation by works but going flat-out to find Him – '*make every effort to enter by the narrow gate*' (**Luke 13:24**). He said I would find if I seek, so I was going to do that.

I wanted a loving relationship with Jesus for the rest of my days. **Psalm 27:4** became my new life verse: *'One thing I ask from the LORD, this only do I seek: that I may dwell in the house of the LORD all the days of my life, to gaze on the beauty of the LORD and to seek Him in His temple.'*

Heaven is a by-product of being in Christ; if we find Jesus, we get eternal life and heaven

---

Seeking Jesus In Sacrifice, Solitude and Separation

How do we seek Jesus?

Seek Jesus in sacrificial alone time with Him. It is not possible to claim that Jesus is my First Love if I don't put aside a special time to be alone with Him one-on-one. I don't do it to get anything from Him or that He should credit me, but just to be in His presence. That is how humans show their highest love to one another and it's even more true with Jesus. This isn't a recipe; it's a relationship!

I spend time with Jesus early morning. You won't find Him in the few minutes between waking up and getting up. That is religious duty, not relationship! It becomes a battle between daily readings, Bible reading and a short prayer. It also competes with whatever else pulls: loved ones, checking messages, weather and news. It is sandwiched between lazy starts and fixed end times (e.g. going to work). Time with God is what gets squeezed out. Instead of glorifying Him as my first priority, He gets my leftovers, even this early in the day.

For me personally it makes little difference if I only get up 15 or 30 minutes earlier (for others this may be different). I try to allow about an hour extra over what I use to for Bible study and prayer. Some days my personal time is relatively short, some days it is longer. Some start their time by listening to worship songs or reading a Biblical devotional (as opposed to a positive thought for the day). Getting up earlier gives the chance to spend unhurried time in God's presence.

I get out of bed and turn off my phone or put it on silent and out of reach! Don't be distracted. Close your door. If you need to, ask others to respect your time. Do whatever it takes to be alone with God.

If Jesus is to be my true First Love then surely He is worth my sacrificial, undivided attention. <u>This is a decision for life, not just while seeking Jesus.</u> This quality time is also core to bearing great spiritual fruit during my life with Jesus.

Some may prefer to get up in the middle of the night, in the total quiet. Yet let it be a planned time, not just when you can't go back to sleep. That is not sacrificial. If, due to your circumstances, your only alone time can be your lunchtime at work, go somewhere you won't be disturbed. It does not matter when, as long as it costs you to be there. There is no substitute for dedicated time with your First Love.

This is personal devotion, listening and speaking time. Bible study and general prayers are different – that can be alone or with others. But my relationship time is in solitude.

I recognise some are not morning people. I love the quiet on both ends of the day. But I don't have the capacity to separate myself fully from the day once I am tired, or even during the day. Someone once wrote about giving God the fresh blossom of the day, and not to make Him wait until the petals have faded. I agree. Also take a lead from **<u>Exodus 34:2-3:</u>** God instructed Moses to come up onto the mountaintop in the morning, alone, and to present himself to

God. Moses, alone with God, in the morning. That is my preferred pattern. If you are that night person, make doubly sure your time does not disappear into the things that distract or into tiredness. If you fall asleep or your mind drifts, then it is perhaps not the right time of day to dedicate to God.

Some may be in a busy, crowded space or household. Others live alone or are retired. Think what being sacrificially separated will mean for you. It is not appropriate to argue someone else has it easier, or others don't understand your circumstances. It isn't a competition; it is between God and you. Decide His priority in your life and live accordingly. My experience is God always rewards those who sacrifice, with more energy, with different types of days, etc. Giving God the very best always results in Him miraculously adding to the day, somehow. Ralph Cushman's poem 'I Met God In The Morning' is worth reading (search the internet). The final verse reads:

So I think I know the secret,
Learned from many a troubled way;
You must seek Him in the morning
If you want Him through the day.

Is your work full-on and you don't have the time? First ask yourself: what is the highest priority in your life? If work comes first, then that may be your chosen first love. Yet if life's circumstances place a heavy demand on you out of necessity, then give your very best to Jesus first. But also think of how you fill the rest of your day – work, sport, socialising, cleaning, social media, news, TV, hobbies, non-essentials. For most people there is plenty of time; just not the priority for Jesus.

Ask God to keep those times interruption free. If you have little time during the week, then create a weekend space to be with Him for longer.

For me, early mornings mean sacrificing the previous late evening. This means cutting the hours doing other things late in the evening. But are we willing?

Spending quality time at the end of the day means before tiredness sets in. I try doing that before I sit down to other things. My daily alarm reminder says 'It Is Time!' Giving Jesus the dregs of my day is worthless. Cherish those times. Don't sacrifice for the sake of sacrificing; God isn't impressed!

'Narrow is the gate'. It requires a 'narrowing down' of my life to be with Him, for the rest of my life. Simplify and be content! It is part of losing our lives to find it. Let us be thankful for the life God gifts us.

Narrowing down my life frees up time for God's purposes. Only a few find Him, because only a few decide He is that important to them

---

Most are satisfied with just being 'a Christian'. Correctly translated this means: religious activity where people serve on their own terms. My experience is that we may learn about Jesus or spend time in His vicinity, but until it costs us and we seek HIM with all our heart, we won't find Him.

Those who don't know what it is to find Him, will forever argue they do know Him. Until He denies them on Judgement Day

---

Jesus may say, 'You associate with Me as the members of an audience with an actor – you know the actor's mannerisms and face from far-off, but you were never introduced or spent time together. The actor doesn't know you, and neither do I!'

To hear about Jesus and learn about Him is cheap. To realise He really lived on the earth, accept He is the Son of God and hear He died for our sins, is cheap. To follow at a distance, as one in the crowd, shout His name, greet Him, speak to Him and cheer when He does something awesome is thrilling but cheap. To give what doesn't really cost me, is cheap. That makes me part of the Many, but not His disciple. Close associations don't count.

His disciples, on the other hand, start the day with Him. They are with Him all the time. They go home with Him in the evening. And they pay the price with Him and for Him.

In human relationships most people will not appreciate you sharing with others intimate thoughts and moments in the relationship, and neither does Jesus. We lose precious value in the relationship when we do. Our motivation for sharing may be our excitement of a specific revelation or moment, but many times it may be laced with pride. Unless God leads you otherwise, refrain from sharing details about your personal time with Jesus.

Over the years I've had encounters with God and words that I've still not shared with anyone, some from a very long time ago. At times God led me to certain actions, promises or understandings, some of which He made clear was for no-one else to know. How do I know this is the case? From a certainty as if I took a resolute decision myself. It is non-negotiable. There were others I could share with someone mature in their faith.

I made the mistake on single occasions of sharing with someone who had no understanding. Not only was it difficult to verbalise, but it cheapened the experience and relationship with God. I realised afterwards it was definitely wrong and the wrong person to share it with. If in doubt, don't share. No-one else may understand why we are so certain that God responded in clear and miraculous ways. These days I treat these moments the same as Paul's words in **Romans 14:23** *'Anything not done in faith* (like being sure to share*) is sin.'* If I am not entirely sure, I keep God's confidence.

Seeking Jesus in Prayer ... And Fasting

Seeking Jesus in prayer meant so many things to me over time. It was such a long journey; God kept the door shut for so long. Yet we are working on a relationship, and that develops daily when we turn up, even if the door doesn't open! I kept recalling His promises that, for everyone who knocks, the door will be opened. Strangely, during all this time God was still using me in His service, sometimes in very obvious ways!

I didn't want to feel better, I wanted Jesus!

Often we just feel down and we want to feel better. This was not the case for me. My prayer life changed completely because for the first time I would not be satisfied with anything less than God Himself. At times I prayed the most agonised prayers. After so many years of seeking, there wasn't space for speaking to anyone else and to hear their advice. It was only God and me. No-one could help me except God Himself.

I was not asking for anything except wanting to be one with Him, typically: Waiting on Him. Asking God to reveal my sinful self to me. Asking His help in repenting because I didn't want anything in my life that dishonoured Him. Asking the Father to help me love Jesus as my First Love. Asking to show me new treasures in His Word. Begging God continually to open my eyes and to give me His Spirit. Pleading with Him to open the door so I could be one with Jesus.

I learned for the first time what it was to not just pray, however sincere and heartfelt. I was so desperate that I fell into fervent prayers sometimes hours on end. I started lying flat on the floor, because even praying on my knees didn't satisfy my desire for God. I often had tears. I got up from my knees daily, still wanting to be on my knees because I felt so unfulfilled. There was a deep desire and yet an emptiness that kept driving me. But I knew, that I knew, that although there was no answer from heaven, I changed so much during those times of no reply from God, it raised my desperation even more.

<u>If God promised I could meet the Creator Himself in person, I would stop at nothing until I found Him in all His glory</u>. I was so determined I was not going to be one of the Many who never met Jesus and I was not going to be left behind when Jesus came for His own.

I was like the two blind men (**_Mat 20:29-34_**) who kept calling out to Jesus loudly, asking Him to have mercy on them. The multitude around them told them to keep quiet but they kept calling even louder '*Lord, Son of David, have mercy on us!*'(**_v31_**). They persisted because they were desperate, and they realised Jesus was the only one who could help them. Jesus asked them '"*What do you want Me to do for you?*"' (**_v32_**). '*Lord, that our eyes may be opened.*' (**_v33_** NKJV). And Jesus had compassion on them and touched their eyes.

Are you desperate for Jesus to open your spiritual eyes? Not just to who He is, but desperate to see the wretch that you are before His holiness and to have Jesus deal with your sins?

One of my prayers I wrote down was '*Lord, please show me what I have not forsaken for You yet. Any sin in the smallest. Any love for the world in its most innocent. Any act of self-will in its simplest and its most natural expression. Any part of my nature. Every moment of my life. Every hidden self-complacency. Every exercise of body, soul and spirit.*' The absence of His Spirit confirmed to me there was more.

For a long time I stopped praying for anything except for the most urgent. I did not want anything else unless I knew I was in a right relationship with Jesus. I was being brought back to seeking first the kingdom of God and His righteousness. For me that meant just seeking Jesus. I truly struggled to pray for anything else.

I wanted a real relationship. I wanted to come to the Father on the basis that He was pleased to hear my prayers, because of my true relationship with His Son. Why would I want to pray to Him as a servant if I could be a son? Yet, coming to God in oneness with Jesus was not possible until I had received His Spirit.

---

*I didn't want to approach God as a slave, who only has a temporary place in the family, but as a son who belongs to it permanently (**John 8:35**)*

This was such a different understanding from my old assumption that I had the Spirit because I believed in Jesus – the assumption of the Christian church. That is so out of kilter with the truth of the Scriptures. When I looked at great men and women of God from the past, their lives were so different to the message we preach today. **Hebrews 11** is of REAL faith. Only this would satisfy me.

I prayed saying to God that, if nothing else came of my faith life, then it would be enough to have found Jesus. Little did I know THAT MEETING JESUS IS THE CROWN, not how I was used afterwards.

Solomon prayed for wisdom, but David, a man after God's own heart (***Acts 13:22***), prayed for 'one thing' – to be in God's presence, forever (***Ps 27:4***)!

Seeking God in prayer (rather than coming with a prayer list) was the most challenging time of my life. *'Agónizomai'.* Agony. Making every effort (***Luke 13:24***) indeed.

But what do you do when you get nothing but emptiness back? Consider seeking Jesus in fasting. Fasting from food, or, if you aren't able to do that, fasting from your normal activities in a normal day. Has He ever been so important that you don't come to Him for any other purpose but just to find Him? *'You will seek Me and find Me, when you seek Me with all your heart'* (***Jer 29:13***).

Finding Jesus is the pursuit of a true life, and it is in the inner room that we agonise and that we find unimaginable riches, love and victory. Develop your relationship with God by speaking to Him about all things, not to persuade Him, but to be persuaded by Him. Get into the habit of a lifetime: ALWAYS PRAY!

Seeking Jesus in The Word

The Bible is the way God communicates the vast majority of His thoughts and truths to us. We look to Him for a word but He has already spoken. He will not entrust personal words to us until we listen to what He already said.

God will lead us to His Truth when we take all of His Word seriously (not just favourite verses). The purpose is not to find out what His words mean to me, but to find what they mean to God! Be careful of Bible study groups where the group is asked what a passage means to them. Yes, God may give us specific direction on a specific issue in a passage (like the man in John MacArthur (American pastor)'s church who was convicted with a single word John read from the Psalms). But our purpose is to find God's meaning.

I appreciate not everyone is a keen reader, yet I find it incomprehensible that someone could claim to be a Christian and that God is their greatest love, and yet they do not read all of His Word, intensively. I heard of one well-known preacher who reads the whole Bible every year and someone else doing it four times a year. And I am sure that would be on top of their normal studies. How many in our churches don't even read the Bible, have never read the whole Bible even once, yet claim Jesus is Lord of their life and the Bible is the Word of God?

If as a human you recorded your most important, deepest messages for your loved ones and they refuse to read them, would you say they return your love for them? Magnify to infinity – That's the lunacy of professing Christians ignoring God's Word.

If you don't yet study the Bible, resolve to study daily for the rest of your life. Perhaps start with a Gospel. Every day, before you read, ask God to guide you by His Spirit. Ask Jesus to reveal Himself to you: His nature, His person, His divinity and His sacrifice so that you can love Him as your First Love. Ask Him daily to show you something you have never seen or realised before and you will be amazed. There is no point in reading the Bible independent of God.

Many idolise the paper the Bible is printed on. No, the WORD is holy. Do whatever it takes to learn and do. The Bible is God's instruction manual and His life messages to you personally. Make every effort to study it, understand it and retain it. That is why God gave it to you. Keep an unblemished Bible if you want, and buy a cheap 'working' Bible to make notes in if that will help you absorb the message! Most in the West can afford an extra Bible (and I would guess most who read this book have several).

Much is made of the primacy of one translation over another, but buy a translation that you understand yet that is accurate. Free translations may be popular but they are not enough for a serious reader. Don't start picking translations apart for what you may consider inaccuracies, when you don't follow the very clear words from every translation!

Seek out the God of the message, believe and do what He says. Any translation will allow you to do that. But saturate yourself with the Bible. Some Bible apps allow you to listen to the Bible. Do it while you travel or walk or do exercise as further background reading.

God's Word explains itself: invariably as you ask God to explain something you don't understand, the Spirit will lead you to another passage that answers your question. Ask the Spirit to lead you. Follow His prompts. The answer may not come immediately, but record your question and start to recognise how God answers your questions. It will give you confidence in the God of the Word and in the Word of God.

Read the detail. Read <u>exactly</u> what God says. Read slowly to receive insight into what God means to communicate (i.e. God's intentional message).

The Bible is infallible because the detail is verifiable. The detail and consistency are what distinguishes it from every other religious book in the world. An excellent example of how the detail of the Bible puts it beyond any other 'sacred writings' in accuracy is the Pool of Bethesda where Jesus healed the lame man (***John 5:1-15***). John recorded the location of the pool and that it had 5 porches '*Now there is in Jerusalem near the Sheep Gate a pool, which in Aramaic is called Bethesda and which is surrounded by five covered colonnades.*' This healing was only mentioned in John. Why mention five porches, it doesn't add to the story! Liberal scholars concluded the details were faulty, that the pool was confused with the

Pool of Siloam or may not have existed at all. Yet in the late 19th century the pool was found and accurately identified 100 years later – a five-sided pool, each covered, near the Sheep's Gate. This was verified through this 'unnecessary detail' that serves as verifiable proof of the accuracy of the Bible as the Word of God. The detail gives us confidence in the message of God's Word and His message. Every word matters!

We must read the Bible with attention to detail because then we will get an understanding of what God is saying to us. For instance, when God adds the word '*if*' in a verse then it means there is a condition: **John 15:10** *'If you keep My commands, you will remain in My love, just as I have kept My Father's commands and remain in His love.'*

If God makes something conditional and we don't meet the condition, then that element does not apply to us!

We can make up our own version of the Bible by ignoring words, passages and warnings and only grab hold of the 'good bits' and the easy interpretations. Yet all of the Bible applies!

The modern church has mastered the art of Eisegesis in Bible interpretation (defined in Wikipedia as *'the process of interpreting text in such a way as to introduce one's own presuppositions, agendas or biases. It is commonly referred to as reading into the text. It is often done to "prove" a pre-held point of concern, and to provide confirmation bias corresponding with the pre-held interpretation and any agendas supported by it'*). In short, we hold a position and use snippets from the Bible to back up our position. Let us get back to detailed reading of what God intended (Exegesis). His intentions cannot be judged by a single verse. The intended meaning is always found in the context of the rest of the Bible.

If a word can have four different meanings, yet only one is consistent with the rest of Scripture, then that is the correct meaning, regardless of how many arguments we may bring that others apply. Take God seriously! Cafeteria Christianity, where we choose interpretations snippets and that suit our cause, is lethal! It's careless to argue for other interpretations when we will be the only losers in the argument!

Realise God is making a call on your life. He shows His divinity through His Word. He proves to you that He exists, He calls you to Himself. Don't let the opportunity go wasted! Seek Jesus in Scripture and you will find Him.

Seeking Jesus in Obedience

In this section, let us each come to Jesus and deal with whatever He points out to us. We are following Him, therefore let us follow in whatever He did or said. Forget about what is needed 'before salvation' and what is part of 'sanctification' afterwards. To the serious follower all of Jesus' words apply, always! This isn't about being perfect, but about a heart fully surrendered to Jesus. Someone who really seeks Jesus will obey, even if it takes time, even if we struggle deeply. Faith, love and obedience have always been the building blocks of the relationship between God and His people. Let's follow in faith!

Obedience was the mark of those who loved God throughout Scripture, and this is still the case today

---

John 14:15-23 is a clear message on how to find Jesus and be filled with the Spirit. Three times in succession Jesus says the one who loves Him, is the one who obeys Him, is the one who loves Him. On this basis Jesus promises to ask the Father to give His Spirit, to show Himself and that They (God) will come and make Their home with us.

This is unmissable: if you want to find Jesus, then do what He says in faith and because He is Lord! There is no salvation for trying to follow his teachings in a works-based faith. Yet there is also no salvation in 'believing in Him' if He is not Lord of my life. 'Lord' means He is the Boss. If we won't obey, then He isn't our chosen Lord, so why would we call Him *'Lord'*? We are our own contradiction. Lord and Saviour go together. If He isn't the one, He won't be the other. Worse still, if He isn't Lord, then the devil is our father. There's no other alternative.

Start with the words of Jesus. Many modern Bibles show them in red, so they are easy to spot! Read the setting and the detail. Live out His words in trust and in loving commitment. It is as clear as day: If we want to find Him, we must obey. That is the mark of someone who chooses Him. God says so!

How do we obey? Dead simple. Stop the wrong, do what is right and make amends for past wrongs as far as we are able.

Here are a few examples:

- When Jesus says don't be angry, then stop being angry! Ask Him to help you but resolutely stop your anger and bitterness. Go out of your way to love, permanently! An angry 'Christian' is disobedient. Jesus is serious when He equates unrepented anger to murder! When God rolls back our easy circumstances and we respond with anger towards disagreeable people or circumstances, then they are not the ones who 'make me into the person I don't want to be', but it exposes my unredeemed self inside. Perhaps you manipulate with cold anger: you don't shout but somehow you get your own back by silences, cold revenge, gossip, etc. Perhaps you withhold love and affection. Stop! If we persist, we will not enter the kingdom of heaven, whatever our confession or the perfection of the rest of our lives! Let's ask Him to help us deal with anger, leave it behind and follow His example of kindness and love instead. Our eternity is at stake!

- Do not judge others. Jesus says we will be judged in the same way and by the same measure. He is referring to hypocritical sins: we are guilty ourselves but judge the sins of others. We must realise our own failings!

- When He says stop lying, then stop lying! Speak the full truth, even if it costs you greatly. Stop exaggerating. Ensure that others know exactly what the truthful situation is. Stop bringing people, or leaving people, under false impressions by speaking half-truths or leaving out details or insinuating, etc. Be known as someone who is truthful. Speak what is positive, otherwise keep quiet. Also don't spread a message that you are not certain is the truth, even using technology. Keep confidences of others.

- Jesus says stop sexual lusting and sexual sin. Take it seriously! Stop watching what you shouldn't. Stop keeping the company that you shouldn't. Stop imagining and relishing in your mind past events or hearing of someone else's exploits. It is said the difference between a look and lust is three seconds. And ensure we are not the reason for someone else's fall by what we do, suggest, flirt, dress, etc.

- Stop lusting after things in a lack of self-control: spur of the moment things to make you feel better – spending money, searching the internet for things to buy, spending time on vain projects and activities, just browsing for places to go, ways to beautify, etc. Fence in your appetites. Do the opposite – be content, encourage others.

- When Jesus says to love your neighbour, then love your neighbour, passionately, fully, without reserve. Stop gossiping or causing dissent. Seek opportunities to do good to others. Don't keep company with people who cause friction and strife. Unless it may genuinely cause problems, make amends where you have caused harm.

- If you have an issue with racism (even jokingly), then stop. Do the opposite. Go out of your way to love the very people you disregard. Befriend them; take their side in what is right, defend them. Race is sacred; God determined it. Who are we to act against the one God created? Ask God's forgiveness and for new insight and love. Stand for what is loving, kind and right. It does not mean to take the side of the offender, but to act righteously before God. Remember also in this time of people migration, God commands us to look after the foreigner. The mission field comes to us, let us evangelise!

- If someone has something against you, go and resolve it. Jesus said, *'Therefore, if you are offering your gift at the altar and there remember that your brother or sister has something against you, leave your gift there in front of the altar. First go and be reconciled to them; then come and offer your gift'* (**Mat 5:23-24**). Do not give reasons for past behaviour, ask their forgiveness. Humble yourself. A proud person will not ask forgiveness.

A brief interlude: it is fascinating how we think we can ask God's forgiveness if we will not even ask forgiveness of the person we harmed. That is being disobedient. This much is clear: if I have harmed someone else, God does not want to hear my further pleas for forgiveness or my requests. He sends me to make peace and ask forgiveness. We are not allowed back until we have done that in a spirit of humility and to put it beyond return. Only then does God accept us back! To leave things for a long time and think God forgot and will just gloss over what happened is an utter fallacy! This is what obedience is about. To refuse means I continue as lord of my own life. This is serious!

- If He says to humble yourself like a little child, then be humble. Ask God to show you your pride, and to break it at any cost. A proud person will not enter heaven. *"<u>God opposes the proud</u> but shows favour to the humble." Submit yourselves, then, to God. Resist the devil, and he will flee from you'* (**<u>Jam 4:6-7</u>** and **<u>1 Pet 5:5</u>**)

- Be careful of being easily offended. It is clear proof of selfishness and pride. We respond because we feel we deserve greater honour, respect or consideration. God's kingdom is for those who humble themselves.

- If you have a forgiveness problem, then forgive. God understands how much we may have been hurt by others. This can be very hard. Yet, we want Jesus to forgive us of all that we have done against Him, thousands of times during our lifetime. Ultimately God will not forgive us if we will not forgive. That is clear from Scripture, even as a part of the Lord's Prayer (*'And forgive us our debts, as we also have forgiven our debtors'*) and after the prayer '<u>But if you do not forgive others their sins, your Father will not forgive your sins</u>' (**<u>Mat 6:10</u>**). We cannot go to heaven if God will not forgive our sins! Forgive to the point of interceding for others and ask God to bless them. Take it to Jesus, ask for His help. Deliberately plead for the other person's life. As you step out to forgive, Jesus gives the grace to forgive and to be set free. Others will still have to answer before God for their actions. Re-read the chapter about hell in Book 1. Hell is so awful that we don't want even our greatest enemies to go there. And we most certainly don't want to be there for our lack of forgiveness!

Many people will speak of forgiveness as the turning point in their relationship with Jesus; when they truly forgave, He opened the door of salvation to them.

- Stop worrying, deliberately. Worry shows our underlying doubt in God Himself, that we do not trust God because we either want our own way, or we do not believe He is able to provide. God takes issue with both! Trust Him for all provision and protection. Step out confidently in God.

- When Jesus says not to be a lover of money, then stop loving money! God does not give it to us to keep and to enrich ourselves. The best way to be rid of the love of money is to give it away until it hurts. Have an open hand. Ask God to show you who needs it. Give freely as you have received. Understand where your 'hard-earned' cash came from: God gives the talents, the ability to work and the gift of opportunity. He can remove all of it in a heart-beat.

- When He says to lend to your <u>enemies</u> when they ask and not to expect anything back or in return, then do so.

- When He says not to resist an evil person, then seek their very best, pray God's blessing over them and leave the outcome to God.

- When He says you are to love Him more than anything else, then place Him first and choose to do what He asks, even if it goes against the wishes of those nearest to you. It will cost you. He will change you. He will also make you an instrument in the lives of others. If it becomes clear you must leave behind a job, a hobby, a relationship or a friendship that comes between you and God, or that it harms your family or another, then make that choice!

- When He says not to deny Him before others, then proclaim Him before others. Be prepared in season and out of season (**2 Tim 4:2**) to give a reason for the hope that is in you (**1 Pet 3:15**). Ask the Spirit to lead you.

This is of course only an introduction to what Jesus commanded. Read Jesus' words for yourself. This is the life that pleases God. It is the life that reflects who He is and how He lived before the Father. He did and said exactly what the Father commanded Him. We must become like Him. This is how you seek to find Him. As mentioned in Chapter 3, I highly recommend Michael Chriswell's *'John 7:17 Challenge'* (www.relentlessheart.com).

Get away from those who say obedience is salvation by works. Stick with what Jesus says

---

We either do what pleases Jesus, or we select the world's ways. We must make up our mind either way. Saying we follow, but doing differently, is to live a lie.

Beware of the Lies

While we seek Jesus, God allows our faith to be tested. The battle from the outside intensifies and we are subject to many attacks and deceptions. If we're not careful, we can be pulled onto a side-track and proceed through the stages of the lies of Satan: hear it, believe it, speak it, live it, teach it. It will direct us away from Jesus and we may become ever more fixed in the fabric of the religiosity.

It is easy to steer clear of profanities and distortions outside the church. Discerning seekers may also easily spot blatant lies within Christianity (yet an alarming number fall for this due to their lack of Bible knowledge and their superficial faith). But be on the look-out for subtle near-truths.

The 99% truth mixed with a deadly 1% lie, peddled even by sincere, professing Christians who just accepted un-Biblical fine-sounding words and arguments of others, or people who question or ignore small details in Scripture. It is a modern day repeat Eve and the serpent in Eden. The serpent deceived Eve by questioning God's motives: *'Did God really say ...?'* (**Gen 3:1**). Eve added words *'and you must not touch it'* (**Gen 3:3**) to God's prohibition of not eating from the tree to make God sound restrictive and unloving.

The hardest battles can be half-truths perpetuated by speakers, authors, leaders and church members, who spread falsehoods unknowingly (I hope). They may have been misled themselves. Their message strays in licentious liberalism, worldliness, cheap salvation and works-based judgementalism that disturb the truth of Scripture. The devil ensures this is in churches across the spectrum. There are small distortions that sow doubt and drive the thinnest wedge, trying to invalidate God's sovereignty and His Word, or question the true Christ.

Be careful when someone offers a word or interpretation that just surprises you a little in how easy it is to follow. A lie widens the small gate and the narrow road and cheapens Jesus and His sacrifice and Lordship: a little license to act more freely because 'we are no longer under the law but under grace'. A surprisingly 'free interpretation' of the Word that you have come to know. Perhaps something that diminishes God's authority just a little. Licence to treat Jesus or the Word with a little less respect through actions, words, behaviour and songs. I've sadly seen things under the banner of trusted organisations that truly scream to heaven. These examples have caused great harm to many who are weak in their faith.

Someone once said to me they 'never really rated Paul very highly', thereby questioning teachings that God sovereignly included in Scripture! How arrogant that some think it is acceptable to criticise God's servants and of the Spirit-inspired Word of God (*'All Scripture is God-breathed and is useful for instruction, for conviction, for correction, and for training in righteousness'* **2 Tim 3:17**).

Some justify their sinful lives and say Jesus didn't teach on an issue. They interpret this silence as His approval or that it's a non-issue. Yet even a basic read of the rest of Jesus' teachings resolves the issue contrary to their interpretation.

On the other end of the spectrum are interpretations resulting in legalism and introducing Old Testament customs (Torah observant, etc). Others use Jesus' Hebrew name ('Yehoshua' or shortened to 'Yeshua') to elevate their brand of Christianity (some genuinely feel the need to address Jesus this way. But He does not take kindly to name-dropping to elevate someone or their brand of faith). Others take major issue with minutiae of translations and call all but the King James Version inaccurate or even 'devil inspired'!

Add to this a whole host of spiritual rabbit trails such as that baptism (which is addressed later) water must be emptied over plants, unused communion wine must drunk, showy parades of the Bible with a procession of pious-looking robed people, that praying without upturned palms won't receive from God, etc, etc. They all add controversy that makes faith in Christ into a religion, dilutes the focus on Jesus and widens the road to include the traditions of men. They may sound harmless or pious, yet it starts the professing church's deadly journey away from Christ.

Beware also of Christians who take liberty in their walk you didn't expect: inappropriate laughter and comments, a little crudeness, a recurring sinful habit, justifying behaviour, a slither between their profession at church and their on-street life. Jesus said *'By their fruit you will know them'* (**Mat 7:16**). Beware of adding to God's Word or altering God's choice of words (e.g. using the word 'brokenness' instead of God's term 'sin' and various alternatives for 'repentance'). A tiny addition or exaggeration may look harmless but is so dangerous – we make God say what we want. Or majoring on minors - taking the smallest element of Scripture, incorrectly interpreted, and even creating a new 'church movement' from it. Scripture says *'Do not go beyond what is written'* (**_1 Cor 4:6_**).

These things are the tiny cracks in the dam wall that lead to its destruction. Beware of the lies! When you seek Jesus, be very careful of worldly side tracks.

We can be around Jesus, speak to Him, speak for Him, reach out to Him with palm branches, sing Hosannas and have emotional tears. Yet until He 'knows' me by His rebirthing Spirit, I too live a lie of eternal magnitude. God is waking us up. Let us not settle for the lie but seek until we find Jesus.

We want Jesus, the one who said *'foxes have holes and birds have nests but the Son of Man has nowhere to lay His head'* (**_Luke 9:58_**). He is seldom where it's comfortable, where messages are easy and where the world applauds. His kingdom is not of this earth (**_John 18:36_**). Beware of the lie that keeps small earthly attachments or human wisdom.

Finally, if you are in proximity to Jesus, if you're related to a true disciple, or you gain from their words, or share in their prayers and see their example of following hard, then beware of the lie of association. We gain nothing from the faith of another except their example and their prayers for us.

How will you seek?

To be awakened by God about our spiritual condition is God's blessing and gift. We think it is shameful to admit we are not reborn but that is the devil's trap. Why care about what others think of your doubts! Salvation isn't an intelligence test or a test of your spiritual insight or of your emotional awareness. The only winners are those who express their honest doubts before God and seek Him until they find Him!

This isn't a 'holiness competition'. It isn't a church right to be saved or a show of weakness if you doubt

---

Only what God says matters. If what others think of us is more important than finding Jesus, then that may cost us eternal life.

Get alone with God. Ask Him to guide you to the True Christ. You may already know what holds you back. God may have brought something to your attention repeatedly. If you think the price of giving up is too great, then ask God to open your eyes to the true cost of not giving up! Deal with things before Him resolutely and quickly. Don't debate.

Be careful of anyone who wants to set your mind at ease about your salvation. Their consolation can be deadly. Get in a regular quiet space with Jesus. Be prepared to stay there as long as it takes, even years if that is how long it takes. Few are really prepared to pay the cost of seeking Him.

How will you know when you have found Jesus and entered in through the narrow gate? You will know beyond a shadow of a doubt. No-one will need to tell you because you will have the true deposit of the Spirit testifying in your heart that you are a child of God. The Spirit will transform your life in unimaginable ways. Someone once said to me *'Even your dog will notice you have been reborn.'* It really is unmissable.

A life without Jesus is not worth living. In His wisdom, God not only decided to bring you into this world, but to bring you to this point of awakening your soul. And how will you respond?

6 The 'Second Call'

Twice Jesus said to Peter: *'Follow Me'*.

Jesus first called Peter in **Mark 1:16-18** *'As Jesus walked beside the Sea of Galilee, He saw Simon and his brother Andrew casting a net into the lake, for they were fishermen. "Come, follow Me," Jesus said, "and I will make you fishers of men." At once they left their nets and followed Him.'*

Jesus' last recorded words to Peter were in **John 21:22** were *'You must follow Me.'*

Let's discover the parallel between Peter's journey and ours.

The First Call

Jesus' first call was with an explanation – *'and I will make you fishers of men'*. The second was clear but without further explanation, just *'You must follow Me.'* At the first call Peter did not know Jesus; he responded because Jesus called. Jesus had something about Him that made Peter leave His nets and follow. The call was to come and find out, see and learn.

By the second call Peter had spent three years in Jesus' presence. During that time Peter had every opportunity to get to know the One he was following. In the mornings he woke up and Jesus was there. Jesus moved visibly forward and Peter followed the daily prompt of the physical Jesus. He was moved primarily by sight. He saw the miracles and heard the words and he remained because Jesus was there.

Peter recognised Jesus as *'the Christ (Messiah) of God'* (**_Luke 9:20_**) and yet he disowned Jesus just before the crucifixion, to save himself. How was that even possible?

After the crucifixion Peter saw Jesus twice. Yet in **_John 21:3_** he said to the other disciples *'I'm going out to fish'* and they went with him. After all he saw and heard his nature remained the same – the fisherman he was by nature.

Now Jesus meets with Peter on the shore. At this third meeting they are again fishing, the same as at the first meeting. The old Peter still blunders in where others fear to tread. But now he is heartbroken because he betrayed Jesus, the one he called 'the Christ of God'. And Jesus restores him lovingly.

Confronted

The encounter of Peter's restoration is in **_John 21_**. *'Simon, son of John, do you truly love Me more than these?'* (**_v15_**) Does Peter love Jesus with an *agape* love, preferring Him over all others, a love that only comes from the Spirit? Does Peter love Him more than his old life and all those around him? Jesus calls Peter by his old name, in the context of his worldly life: *'Simon, son of John'*. Not the new 'Peter' (the Rock). Do you love Me <u>more than</u> your worldly calling and your worldly friends? Peter replies: *'Yes Lord, you know that I love you'* (I love you dearly like a friend, a *phileo* love). <u>He had high regard and affection for Jesus</u>. *Note; Peter was honest about his deep friendship love for Jesus. He didn't pretend to have an agape love. This is key to moving forward with Jesus, honest admission, not pretence.* Jesus replies with a new call *'Feed My lambs'*. Come away from your old life to a new calling. <u>Lose your worldly life</u>, instruct the babes in faith.

Jesus asks again (**_v16_**) *'Do you truly love Me?'*, loving Him as the first choice, an *agape* love. This time Jesus does not compare the love with *'more than these'*, but he still calls him *'Simon, son of John'* – the man with an earthly vision. This time it is about Peter himself – do you love Me above all? *'Yes Lord, you know that I love you'* – I dearly love You as a friend, a *phileo* love. *Again the same honesty; he was broken by his denial and has no pretence left. 'Take care of My sheep.'* Care for them, direct them, take up the office of a shepherd.

Jesus asks a third time *'Simon, son of John, do you love Me?'* Now Jesus uses the same word as Peter 'dearly love Me as a friend', a *phileo* love. In the first two questions Jesus was asking about Peter's deep, preferential, God-inspired love for Him, but this time He meets Peter where he is - 'like a friend'. And now Peter responds that Jesus knows all things and that He already knows that Peter loves Him like a dear friend. And Jesus responds *'Feed My sheep'*. Feed the fully-grown.

Then Jesus restores Peter.

Peter's Second Call

The first call was for Peter to get to know Jesus. He invited Peter to come and see, learn who He is and hear His words.

Then comes the second call: *'You must follow Me'*. Now Peter knows what is at stake and he is challenged. He saw how Jesus was persecuted and he met with Him as the Risen Lord. He heard and saw first-hand the cost of following Christ.

Jesus' second call is different from the first. The cross has entered the relationship and now it is serious.

Our Second Call

Our journey is most often similar to Peter's. Jesus calls. We begin to follow Him, learn about the One we are following and about the cost of following. Then we are awakened – Jesus 'calls again' and we must make a deep heart decision. It is deadly serious because our decision has eternal consequences.

We may have followed Jesus for a long or a short time. But following, even closely and for a long time, even as a senior church leader or preacher, is not rebirth or salvation. By now the difference between religion and salvation should be clear, we have covered it many times: I must meet Jesus in person.

How do we respond? Do we die to ourselves, take up our cross and follow? Or do we remain where we are and who we are, choose to live our lives as disciples but never become HIS disciples? The words of Christ are clear: *'if you love your father or mother more than Me, you are not worthy of Me ...'* (**_Mat 10:37_**).

In effect Jesus is now saying: 'You've seen Me, you heard My words, now you know the cost. It is time to make up your mind. Are you in, or are you out? Are you abandoned to Me, forsaking all else, or are you staying religious as you are? Unless you leave your life and follow Me, this time for good, you will lose the little revelation you gained about Me and My life. You cannot stay on the fence, a little in and a little out, mostly living for yourself but claiming association with Me.'

Jesus understands when we start out in sincere 'phileo' love, but it isn't salvation. The cross is between a 'phileo' friendship and a saving 'agape' love relationship

---

Good intentions and paying cheap lip service are deadly because they lull us into a false sense of security. This is serious: we must take a clear-cut decision whether or not to take up the cross and follow Him (**_Mark 8:34_**) and come and die to ourselves (*'whoever loses his life for My sake and for the Gospel will gain it'* (**_Mark 8:35_**).

The cross is not inconvenient hand luggage. It has sharp edges and nails and no-one else helps us carry it. To pick it up means death to myself and the world. Once we pick it up we stay with it and it stays with us. We pick it up and God allows us to enter the small gate and we keep carrying it to the end. Or we leave it and remain in our comfortable broad way life of religion and drift away from outside the small gate, even while we remain inside the earthly church.

As it was with Peter, so our call now becomes life-altering too, because the cross enters our relationship with Jesus too.

Onwards!

God is encouraging you onward. Jesus spoke of the fig tree that hadn't borne fruit for three years. The land owner wanted to cut it down (***Luke 13:6-9***). Are you in that year's grace period? Has the Gardener been fertilising and digging around your tree? We must be very careful about resisting God's call. Throughout history people hardened their hearts, and at some point, God hardened their hearts. We cannot assume there will be a next opportunity.

He calls you a 'second time' (perhaps many more by now). You understand more. You heard His words, He showed you who He is and what He does. You spent time in His presence.

God Calls Your Name!

Now is the time for real change. Come, be born a Peter.

Until we are reborn a Peter, we remain a Simon. The birth may be painful and the process may take time. Once we take this decision, we stick with it. Even if the Spirit is not gifted to us for 20 years, we continue because our decision is deep and final. Jesus is worth it and we make every effort to enter by the narrow gate. Not by works, but by resolute abandon and determined following!

It is time to *'seek first the kingdom of God and His righteousness'*. Nothing else is more important. Put all of your life second, even on hold if you must. It is time to put your hand to the plough and not look back (***Luke 9:62***). Like Elijah, burn your yokes and slaughter your oxen. Let everyone know where you stand (***1 Kings 19:19-21***). Break with your old life permanently.

God often called someone's name twice to get their attention: *'Abraham, Abraham!'* (***Gen 22:11***). *'Moses, Moses!'* (***Ex 3:4***). *'Samuel, Samuel!'* (***1 Sam 3:10***). *'Martha, Martha!'* (***Luke 10:41***).

Today God calls your name twice to get your attention too. It is meaningful and significant. He calls loudly and He says 'choose'!

Understand that you are choosing for all eternity. You are not choosing heaven; you are choosing Jesus because He alone is worthy.

You are choosing to let go of this life and its temporary but deceiving trinkets, and to grab hold of King Jesus and His way. How do you decide?

'This day I call the heavens and the earth as witnesses against you that I have set before you life and death, blessings and curses. Now choose life ...'
(Deut 30:19)

---

7 Water Baptism

Until now we have not talked about water baptism, a significant event in the life of every believer in Jesus Christ. This chapter covers elements that will not apply to all readers but it is included due to the wide-ranging practices in the church. The chapter is therefore divided into a discussion that applies to baptism in general, followed by a section on those who have been baptised as infants or small children or have already or want to bring their children for baptism (including the concept and selection of godparents), and finally options for those who wish to bring their children forward formally in a Biblical ceremony. Readers who are only involved in or choose believers' baptism can therefore omit the last two sections of the discussions as they will not apply to them.

Water baptism is either the worldly church's religious act that demotes it to little more than a superstitious ceremonial rite, or a thoughtful joyous act and public declaration of our intent to follow Christ. As has been our approach in all our discussions, this is not a theological exposé on baptism, but to establish the clear intention of God that He communicates to us in Scripture for those who believe. We therefore look at water baptism through the eyes of faith of someone who seeks the full Truth of God, rather than through the eyes of the Christian religion.

My Own Baptism

I would like to share my own path of baptism before we start. I was baptised as a baby of two then unsaved parents. It was a religious ritual with much emphasis on the baptism frock handed down through generations. It took place in what I now know to be a dead large 'state' reformed denomination. After 12 years of Sunday school and certificates I was confirmed, along with all others in my year.

I was married in the same denomination (made possible by church membership through baptism and confirmation). I baptised my own children in the same tradition, made possible by my own church membership through infant baptism and confirmation. It was unthinkable (heretical) that one would leave children unbaptised (or even be baptised as an adult!)

Many years after I became a disciple of Jesus I insisted on being baptised by full emersion, having been convicted by the Spirit. My new church was unwilling to 're-baptise' me as it would break church rules. I could therefore only be baptised outside of a normal service or my 're-baptism' in a formal service would be under the banner of 'baptismal regeneration' which I could not accept. I was therefore baptised privately with just five people present.

I have met the True Jesus Christ (as opposed to the religion of Christianity) and I look back in disbelief at these worldly church systems that have greater concern for its own rules than for the commands of the God they profess to serve.

Water Baptism General Discussions

The Place of Baptism Within Faith

The decision to be baptised in water is not to be taken lightly. It is a sacred thing before God and it does great harm to the name of Jesus if the evidence of our lives contradicts our public confession. If we doubt our willingness to surrender all, then rather wait. Jesus told the Church in Laodicea He wished they were either hot or cold, but because they are lukewarm He was going to spit them out of His mouth (**_Rev 3:15-16_**). God hates our lack of fire for Jesus.

Baptism is a physical act with deep spiritual significance. There is a certain memory of the day we openly confessed before others and a deep blessing of God. We call to witness the Almighty God for our intention to follow Jesus for the rest of our lives. Baptism is a physical act by which we identify with the death, burial and resurrection of Christ. It is the outward witness of a permanent voluntary break with the old, choosing Jesus above all and to follow as He says.

God is able to affect us in a profound way through the waters of baptism. It was not without reason that the Holy Spirit descended on Jesus immediately after His baptism.

I remember reading the book 'I Dared to Call Him Father' by Bilquis Sheikh, a Muslim woman who found Jesus as her Saviour. Her relatives came to dissuade her from converting to Christianity (they didn't understand that she found the Truth of Christ; to them she was abandoning Islam for another religion). Yet she was desperate to make her choice of Christ permanent and beyond return. She knew this was through baptism. In the absence of someone to baptise her, she filled the bath and went under in complete immersion. (Note: self-baptism is definitely not anywhere in Scripture, however I am sure God saw this woman's heart, and for her it also put her decision beyond return.) This signalled to her family that there was no going back for her. Baptism is also the way many from other religions (Hinduism, Buddhism, etc) make their decision final and beyond return. Families and friends will still try to dissuade, but once they are baptised, this is considered the final break and they disown and persecute the new Christian.

We must approach our water baptism with this gravity. It is a personal statement of a final break with the old life and a choice for Christ. Is that how you understand it too? Is that how seriously you approached your baptism? Anything less than full conviction and commitment is meaningless before God.

Is Baptism Essential for the Believer?

In a word, YES. When we read the command to be baptised, together with His words that the sign of true followers is that they obey everything He commanded, this puts the requirement of baptism beyond question. Rather than refer to baptism as a sacrament we should practice it for what it is: An ordinance. It is an authoritative decree, command or order from God by the words of Jesus.

Even from the start of John the Baptist's ministry, baptism was directly linked to repentance (**Mat 3:11**, **Mat 3:6**, etc). Throughout the Gospels people were being baptised in an expression of their faith and their repentance.

Jesus' command to baptise and to be baptised appears in both accounts of the Great Commission: '*Therefore go and make disciples of all nations, baptising them in the name of the Father and of the Son and of the Holy Spirit, and teaching them to obey everything I have commanded you...*' (**Mat 28:19-20**) and '*He said to them, "Go into all the world and preach the gospel to all creation. Whoever believes and is baptised will be saved, but whoever does not believe will be condemned*' (**Mark 16:15-16**). We also find it in **Acts 2:37-38** '*When the people heard this, they were cut to the heart and said to Peter and the other apostles, "Brothers, what shall we* do?" 'Peter replied, "Repent and <u>be baptised</u>, every one of you, in the name of Jesus Christ for the forgiveness of your sins. And you will receive the gift of the Holy Spirit"'. There are more references, such as **_Acts 18:8_**, but these will suffice.

To conclude then: Jesus commands us to be baptised. We profess Him as Lord; therefore it is our direct command. We have a choice: we either embrace Him as Lord and Saviour, or we don't. Baptism is one of the very first steps of obedience for a new follower. The Spirit will remind a true follower of the need to be baptised. If we disobey on this point, it speaks volumes of the truth of our death to self and faith in Christ. Our refusal is a sign of a rebellious heart, not a surrendered heart.

Does Baptism Save?

Baptism in itself does not save, nor are any sins forgiven as a result of baptism alone. Verses on water baptism and salvation always stand in the context of all other passages regarding salvation. In the same way that John 3:16 isn't freestanding proof that 'just faith' (as we understand it) is required for salvation, so we can also not say that baptism in itself washes away sins. Sin is only washed away at the same time as salvation is given. All the core elements of salvation must be present together for us to have the complete picture.

- Billions, baptised as infants or adults, still live godlessly or religiously, are unsaved and therefore still end up in hell.
- It is un-Biblical to say the 'original sin' inherited from Adam is forgiven when we baptise a baby, hence the practice. This is nowhere to be found in Scripture and is purely an invention of the Catholic Church.
- It is also un-Biblical to say that we can claim people for God by baptising them. God decides sovereignly who He

saves. Our action of baptising someone cannot take another's decisions to follow, to believe and to surrender to Jesus. Yet we should boldly in intercede for others.

Meaning of the Word 'Baptise'

The original Greek word for 'baptism' is *baptizó*, meaning to dip (even repeatedly), sink (like a sunken ship), submerge, or plunge. It means to be fully submerged under water. *Baptizó* stands in contrast with *rhantizó* which means to sprinkle or to cleanse ceremonially by sprinkling.

In the New Testament **John 3:23** gives a good indication of God's intention on how to baptise '*Now John also was baptising at Aenon near Salim, <u>because there was plenty of water</u>, and people were coming and being baptised*'. With the baptism of Jesus His full emersion is evident in **Mark 1:10** '*Just as Jesus was <u>coming up out of the water</u>, He saw heaven being torn open and the Spirit descending on Him like a dove*'. And when Philip baptised the Ethiopian eunuch in **Acts 8:36** '*As they travelled along the road, they came to some water and the eunuch said, "Look, here is water. What can stand in the way of my being baptised?*"' '*Some water*' does not mean 'a little water', but some translations speak of '*they came onto a certain water*'. There was enough water, for what was understood by all, full immersion. If only a sprinkling was required, a small amount of water from a drinking canteen would have sufficed.

In order to appease the later church's religious practice of sprinkling (especially infants), the word *baptizó* was not properly translated into 'plunge', 'dip' or 'submerge', but transliterated into 'baptise'. As a result, John the Plunger (or John the Dipper) became John the Baptist. This helped to 'legitimise' un-Biblical ceremonial sprinkling, and the practice continues amongst many denominations today.

God's clear intention in Scripture for baptism is by full immersion. Jesus Himself is our example. *Baptizó* means to immerse. There is no other baptism. Is this distinction important? Yes! If we take liberties with how we baptise, we will also take liberties with who we baptise and decide for ourselves the meaning and place of baptism.

Who Must Be Baptised, On What Basis?

<u>Paedobaptism v Credobaptism</u>

We will spend a brief moment on infant baptism as it will be discussed in greater detail later in this chapter.

Paedobaptism is the religious rite of baptising infants. This covers any children who are brought for baptism on the basis of their parents' (or that of others) wish and decision, rather than their own clear understanding and decision to follow Christ.

Credobaptism is the baptism of disciples who put their faith in Jesus and decided to follow Him and be baptised. This may include children with sufficient insight to take the decision for themselves (rather than being strongly directed towards baptism by others).

The fact that water baptism is only to be enacted on those who decide to follow Jesus is evident especially from **<u>Matthew 28:19-20</u>** '... *make disciples of all nations, <u>baptising them</u>* ...'. Jesus' clear intention is that baptism is for <u>disciples</u> (*baptising <u>them</u>* [disciples]). This intent is further noticeable in several accounts in Acts (typically **<u>Acts 2:41</u>**, **<u>8:12</u>**, **<u>8:13</u>**, **<u>9:18</u>**). We will discuss the implications for infant baptism later in the chapter.

Baptism and the Journey of Faith

Where does baptism fit into the faith journey of the believer? It comes after the person took for themselves the decision to follow Christ.

Scripture mentions two different statuses at baptism: the decision to follow has been taken but the Spirit is not received yet (e.g. **Acts 2:37-41**), or the person received the Spirit at their full surrender and their baptism happens afterwards (e.g. Cornelius in **Acts 10:44-48**). Either way baptism follows the decision to follow, regardless of our Spirit status at the time.

On What Basis?

What 'yardstick' may be best to determine the person's readiness for baptism? Some Scripturally sound churches encourage baptism at the point of the decision to follow Christ, others only after further teaching on discipleship and the cost of following, and some at evidence of repentance. The latter seems more in keeping with the intention of Scripture (**Acts 26:20, Mat 3:8, Heb 6:4-12**). Paul said in **Acts 26:20** 'I preached that they should repent and turn to God and demonstrate their repentance by their deeds'. Can the person testify how their life changed since they decided to follow Christ (breaking with specific sin, making restitution, asking forgiveness, stepping out in faith in specific situations, etc)?

Who Can Baptise, Where, How?

Who Can Baptise?

People generally assume only church leader or similar can baptise, and only in a church. In many denominations church leaders are licensed to act on behalf of the church and unlicensed members cannot baptise on their own (but may assist). In the true Body of Christ any Spirit-filled believer can baptise. Jesus' command to make disciples and to baptise was given to every believer and not limited to leaders only.

Where to Baptise?

Baptism can take place anywhere that it is appropriate to do so and that allows for full immersion. We are being baptised into the body of believers; therefore it is right to be baptised in their presence where possible, with their prayers and their support. If you are not able to find such a church and wish to be baptised, there is nothing that prevents baptism elsewhere, by a Spirit-filled believer, with single people in attendance.

How?

It is important for the baptiser to ascertain to the best of their knowledge the aptness of baptism: to confirm the person's correct understanding of what faith in Jesus as Saviour and Lord means.

It is appropriate to repeat the basics tenants of faith in Christ and to ask the person to confirm that this is the reason for their decision to be baptised. It is a solemn promise before God to leave the old life behind and to believe, love and follow Christ and His words above all else.

As for the words spoken over the person, Jesus commanded us to baptise '*in the name of the Father and of the Son and of the Holy Spirit*' (**Mat 28:19**).

Some baptisers pray over the person to receive the Spirit immediately after baptism once out of the water. This is entirely Biblical, although it is not the prayer of the baptiser that determines if the Spirit is received or not. Water and spirit baptism are two entirely separate events, even if they may take place in close proximity. The one action is done by man and the other by God. He gives His Spirit with His perfect knowledge of the heart condition of that person: whether they truly repented and are fully surrendered to His Lordship.

Water Baptism and Spirit Baptism

Salvation seldom happens at confession of faith (otherwise Jesus could not have said of the Many [who will all have professed faith in Him because they called Him 'Lord, Lord'] 'I never knew you'. Therefore in practice water baptism takes place after the decision to follow rather than only after the person is reborn by the Spirit. Admittedly some in Acts received the Spirit first, and they were subsequently baptised in water after God already showed He accepted them, but this will be the exception.

It can be misleading to claim that the newly baptised has been 'baptised into the family of God'. We may be baptised into the 'church family' (a socio-religious structure), but that has no eternal merit in itself. We are either reborn into the family of God, or not.

Baptism and the Many

Space does not permit for a full discussion on this topic, yet I want to put a wider issue into context, one I believe may be directly linked to the water baptism practiced in many churches, and how the membership of churches is determined:

This wonderful gift of God has been abused by earthly churches for many years. Yet it was entirely predictable: the earthly church has largely ceased to be a body of Spirit-filled believers and become a religious gathering. Churches that baptise ('christen') infants who have no faith, declare them to be a part of God's or the church's 'family'. This in turn often converts into a lifetime of dead membership and of many who are 'sincerely' lost.

It is outside of the narrow gate of salvation in Jesus that we make a public confession. This is where we declare to the world our new association with Jesus and our firm intention in public confession and promise, to follow Him all the days of our lives. We do God's name a great injustice if we stop following and we will be ridiculed: *'Suppose one of you wants to build a tower. Won't you first sit down and estimate the cost to see if you have enough money to complete it? For if you lay the foundation and are not able to finish it, everyone who sees it will ridicule you, saying, "This person began to build and wasn't able to finish"'* (**Luke 14:28-30**). Yet it isn't our confession and intentions that save, but God's sovereign grace.

If you are truly intent on following Christ and you have not yet been baptised as a believer, then why not? I am convinced many people who are struggling to overcome sinful patterns and with truly finding Jesus are ones who may be sincere but unbaptised as followers. When they do humbly come to be baptised in public association with Him, many may be so struck by the profound mystery of baptism that they are finally released and find the true love and salvation of God.

Baptising Infants and Children

This section covers those who have been baptised as an infant or young child (regardless of age now). In the next section we will concentrate on typical issues for those who are considering baptising a child or have baptised children in the past.

Origins of Infant Baptism / Christening

The practice of infant baptism was cemented into church practice around A.D. 200 – 400, the main protagonist being the Catholic Church. It was later adopted by most of the main denominations, most of which can be considered a form of state church. The alternative term of 'christening' probably best describes the wrong understanding of the role of baptism – it does not make someone a Christian (perhaps in name, but as for salvation, it has no effect in itself).

Bible Texts Used to Support Infant Baptism

Were one to question supporters of infant baptism, many will say an infant is included in the 'family of God' at baptism because of the use of the words 'and his household' in some accounts of baptisms in the book of Acts. Let us look at typical texts that may be quoted.

The Philippian Jailer's Household

Some use the conversion and baptism of the Philippian jailer's household in **_Acts 16:25-34_** to justify baptising infants: *'He then brought them out and asked, "Sirs, <u>what must I do to be saved</u>?" They replied, "<u>Believe in the Lord Jesus</u>, and you will be saved – <u>you and your household</u>." Then <u>they spoke the word of the Lord to him and to all the others in his house</u>. At that hour of the night the jailer took them and washed their wounds; then immediately <u>he and all his household were baptised</u>. The jailer brought them into his house and set a meal before them; he was filled with joy <u>because he had come to believe in God – he and his whole household</u>'.*

When we read the full passage rather than a snippet ('*you and your household*'), the meaning becomes clear. It reads '*believe in the Lord Jesus and you will be saved*'. This account was about people who heard, understood and believed (v34), they were subsequently all baptised (v33) and filled with joy (v34). No infant or small child would qualify. This event was about the jailer's whole household, which included household staff who could understand. To make the intention clearer the passage above could be restructured as follows: *'What must I do to be saved?' 'You and each one of your whole household, believe in the Lord and each of you will be saved according to their own faith'. Then all in his household who heard this and believed were baptised immediately and were filled with joy.*

'To You and to Your Children'

Others refer to Peter's words in **Acts 2:38–39**: *'Repent, and be baptised, every one of you, in the name of Jesus Christ for the forgiveness of your sins; and you shall receive the gift of the Holy Spirit. <u>For the promise is to you and to your children</u>'*. A basic reading of the text shows the error of the assumption: REPENT, and then be baptised – the promise of salvation (the Spirit) applies to everyone who comes on this basis. This does not say to include young children in baptism.

Lydia and Her Household

Acts 16:13-15 reads *'... One of those listening was a woman from the city of Thyatira named Lydia, a dealer in purple cloth. She was a worshipper of God. The Lord opened her heart to respond to Paul's message. When <u>she and the members of her household were baptised</u>, she invited us to her home. 'If you consider me a believer in the Lord,' she said, 'come and stay at my house.' And she persuaded us'*. Again we read about a household being baptised, again Lydia was 'one of those listening'. The same argument: listening and understanding cannot be said to apply to infants.

Cornelius, His Family and His Friends

The final Scriptural example is Cornelius and his family and friends in **_Acts 10_**. Let us look at elements of the account to support the Peter's decision to baptise the household of Cornelius.

Firstly, Acts 10. Verse 2 says '*He* [Cornelius] *and all his family were devout and God-fearing ...*' which means they were of an age and understanding to be devout and God-fearing, not that infants and young children were present.

Next comes a better description of who was present at the meeting with Peter. **_Acts 10:24_** reads '*Cornelius was expecting them and had called together his relatives and close friends*'. Then **_Acts 10:33_** '*Now we are all here in the presence of God to listen to everything the Lord has commanded you to tell us*'. After that **_Acts 10:44_** '*While Peter was still speaking these words, the Holy Spirit came on all who heard the message*'. Lastly **_Acts 10:47_** '"*Can anyone keep these people from being baptised with water? They have received the Holy Spirit just as we have.*" *So he ordered that they be baptised in the name of Jesus Christ*'.

All these verses confirm that everyone in the wider family and friends heard and believed for themselves, and God confirmed their faith by the Spirit. Water baptism was administered on their confession and God's seal of their authentic faith. This did not include children who had no understanding. From the start of the church in Acts the Spirit was not given without faith that satisfied God.

Does Baptism Replace Circumcision?

Many Christians who bring a child to baptism do so because they think it is the New Covenant replacement of circumcision. The logic is probably that, as circumcision linked an Israelite/Jew to the Old Covenant, so baptism joins a baby or adult to New Covenant salvation in Christ. This is un-Biblical: Baptism is not the manner to access the New Covenant. It is also wrong to assume family units are included in the New Covenant. Salvation is individual and by personal faith alone and baptism follows the same path.

Signing With a Cross

Some churches encourage signing the forehead with a cross, with a finger dipped in the baptismal water (normally by parents, godparents and even grandparents). We already discussed that infant baptisms are not Biblical, yet further, why do we want to add to the baptism Jesus ordained? The practice may appear spiritual, but let us stick with what is Biblical and leave man-made rituals alone. Our blessing lies in God and what He gives, without adding to His commands.

Paedobaptism is pseudo-baptism!

Spiritual Status of a Baptised Infant

We must ask ourselves what would be the purpose before God of baptising infants. They may be baptised in the church's eyes, but are they in God's, and what is their spiritual status?

Say two babies, one baptised and the other not, die. Could we imagine God would send one to hell and the other to heaven just because one's parents asked that water be sprinkled on its forehead? What if they lived to be 12, is the one forever saved and the other damned because of some religious rite of their parents? Surely not! We don't know the eternal status of any infant or unborn baby who dies; God has not revealed that to us in Scripture. But we do know that they are in the hands of a righteous, loving God. Whatever He does is perfect and right, regardless of water sprinkled over them or not.

The outstanding question is, then, if baptism on its own doesn't save an infant (and it doesn't), what is the purpose of their baptism? Those churches have made it into a hollow religious rite that does great harm to true faith in Christ.

Baptism of Long-standing Followers

What about long-time followers, baptised as infants: Should they be baptised? Some denominations call this 're-baptism' in derogatory terms, others refuse to 're-baptise'.

Baptism without repentance, faith and the decision to follow is not valid. The paedobaptised person is unbaptised before God. Scripturally (our only true basis) such a person should be baptised, i.e. their first baptism! Even if someone is 80 and had been 'religiously' following Jesus, His command still applies. If a church does not support 're-baptism' then find another church or believer who will. If you are serious about Jesus, do it.

Being baptised after a long time in the church makes a profound difference to the person who is being baptised – it brings a new seriousness to their faith and life with Christ that never existed before. Baptism is indeed a physical act with great spiritual significance! Once we bow to God's ways and commands we find new life. Yet, how many will humble themselves before God and man in this way? Sadly, few!

'I Am Satisfied with My Baptism'

I have spoken to several people about believer's baptism who replied 'I am satisfied with my (infant) baptism'. I suspect their reason is generally one of the following:

- It may be out of allegiance to a loved one who 'christened' them. Out of love and respect for that person they won't question the actions of those they hold in high esteem.

- People trust their church's leadership to be correct in all things religious. If the church approves and practices infant baptism then the church knows best and is correct.

- Some are just unwilling to be 'humiliated' (rather than humbling themselves) in this manner. They consider themselves Christian already and don't see the point.

- Some view baptism (with confirmation later) as a religious ritual requirement which they already satisfied with their infant baptism. It gives them rights within the church already, so they don't see the need for believer's baptism.

- Still others come from religious families where infant baptisms are the norm. To question it is to question the faith of the family. Some are actively dissuaded – it 'brings shame' on the name of an upstanding religious family. Note: It is also uncanny how many times a family member or a close friend who has no faith and hardly attends church, becomes the driving force behind a child's baptism. This is superstition and custom. How sad that well-meaning parents may be persuaded to baptise due the insistence of an unbeliever to honour their wishes!

- A final point, although not quite in keeping with the heading of this section, is those who were never baptised and feel it is a mere formality or just a point of obedience. They don't see the need to comply because they argue they believe already, and 'faith alone is required for salvation'.

Do any of these reasons and arguments stand up to Biblical scrutiny? No, and for the following reasons:

Firstly, Jesus did exactly what the Father commanded. He was baptised by John in obedience to the Father ('*Jesus replied, "Let it be so now; it is proper for us to do this to fulfil all righteousness"'* **Mat 3:15**). Jesus is our example – when we claim we believe, then we follow as Jesus commanded!

Secondly, it is clear throughout the New Testament that to be baptised was an automatic imperative for a repentant believer, not as a rule but a desire of a true follower. They want to make their association with Jesus public and permanent. We can also not argue we've followed for so long that baptism does not matter anymore. It is always of utmost importance before God. Obedience does not have an expiry date.

Thirdly, and on a practical level, our faith is always about God's glory, not for our benefit. Whether I am satisfied with my infant baptism or not has no value before God. Only God's judgement matters. His position is clear – He commands faith baptism. He does not recognise our worldly human traditions.

Let us be careful not to use our own satisfaction or to measure our goodness before God. Let us only measure ourselves in the light of God's Word. This includes baptism.

The Sprinkled Adult

What if an adult had come in faith and repentance, their reason for their 'baptism' was Biblical, yet they were 'sprinkled'? Should they be 're-baptised' by full immersion? If it was me, on my own conviction, I would. Why? Because I believe it honours God in a Biblical manner. Is it essential? Perhaps not. Make it a matter of personal conviction before God.

What if someone who hasn't yet taken the serious decision to follow Jesus in faith and repentance, was sprinkled or baptised to satisfy a church requirement in order to be married in the church, etc? In faith terms the baptism and sprinkling were meaningless because it wasn't in true repentance and faith in Jesus. When such a person does then become a serious follower, let them be baptised.

Infant Baptism and Confirmation

In churches where infant baptism is practiced it is often followed by confirmation later in life, perhaps after a formal doctrine program, so that a person is deemed fit for membership. This gives access to communion (the Lord's Supper) and voting and membership rights. In the case of a paedobaptised person who subsequently made a decision to follow Christ, churches may direct them to be confirmed. <u>So, at exactly the point the person decides to give their life to Jesus and follow Him seriously and needs Biblical baptism, and when the church should be baptising that person in joy, many churches refuse to baptise on account of their tradition.</u> Some churches may agree to baptise someone informally or outside the church building, so long as it isn't 'official'. What a travesty before God! And all this to protect un-Biblical practices of the organised church! This is sad and scandalous!

Confirmation is the religious fabrication to deal with baptism of those who decided to follow seriously after paedobaptism. To justify this practice some officials call confirmation 'the completion of infant baptism'. For those who insist on being baptised (in the church), there is yet another religious invention: 'baptismal regeneration'. What falseness!

None of these man-made inventions have a place in the true church. If someone must be confirmed as a member of a church, then keep it away from faith for salvation. In Scripture there is no 'completion of baptism' or 'baptismal regeneration'.

Why don't we 'just' uphold Biblical Truth?!

Those who officiate over these events must also realise they will give an account before God. How truly sad that, at the very time someone decides to follow Christ for the rest of their lives, the earthly church interferes with falsehood to justify its earthly practices.

Options for Infants and Children

What options are available to godly parents with a true desire to mark the advent of a child before God and in the presence of other believers? There is no prescribed way but there are two commonly used avenues:

Thanksgiving and Blessing

It is good and God-honouring for parents to bring their child to the church in an act of thanksgiving. It is also good for parents to ask the church to pray a blessing over the child, for the spiritual life of the child and for each person to be reminded to pray for the child as he/she grows up.

Dedication

Dedicating a child to God is another option. In fact, believing parents should be dedicating their children to Christ in a personal capacity anyway, whether in the church also or not.

Perhaps the clearest example of a dedication in the Bible was Hannah's dedication of Samuel (***1 Sam 1:21-28***). It does not mean we leave our children behind to serve in the church as Hannah left Samuel! But it is a measure of our own faith whether we entrust our children to God in absolute faith, that we bring them up for the sole purpose of glorifying God through Christ. That should be our prayer regardless, but this act of dedication puts our decision to entrust God with our child's entire life and future in the forefront of our minds, just as it should be! If such a faith is true for parents and they entrust their own lives to God's care, then they will want their children to share in that same surrender. It is also wholesome to realise that children are God's gift to us, being entrusted with their guardianship, but that God is ultimately the giver of that life. We are responsible before Him how we bring the child up for His glory.

The Question of Godparents

In a true believers' church the responsibility for prayer and discipling support for children should not only rest with the parents or guardians of a child, but also with the church. Some churches do this well by taking the precious children on as their co-responsibility, bearing them up before God, to support and pray for the child and their parents and to help and guide the child by their teaching and their example.

Appointing godparents is a human convention since it isn't mentioned in the Bible. It may be perfectly acceptable, provided we recognise it isn't Biblical and that it does not become part of a worldly religion. It is very easy to disappear down man-made religious rabbit trails that can lead us astray.

The practice of choosing godparents is varied. In the world it is mostly a secular wish for 'stand-in guardians' in the event something befalls the parents (though they don't normally have legal status without further legal documentation).

Some church parents genuinely desire godly godparents to support the child's spiritual journey with prayer and direct interaction. This can be a formal way to recognise this desire.

Unfortunately many choose relatives or friends who have no true relationship with Christ. Instead the person is being 'honoured' by their selection, rather than for spiritual support and guidance. Surely the correct way to deal with this is not by cheapening something that is intended to support the child spiritually by selecting someone who does not believe!

A further issue to consider is that many churches require parents and godparents to make promise on behalf of the infant who cannot speak for themselves! This is obviously entirely without Biblical merit; there is no vicarious decision-making or salvation before God.

A final issue that often goes unnoticed: As part of the baptismal ritual godparents are often asked to declare their own faith. Many who do not have faith in Christ themselves therefore make a false declaration and promise before God, not thinking of the gravity of their words. They may think of it as merely a part of a formality, yet it is a grave thing to make a promise before God if we do not intend to follow it through.

Parents, think deeply and seriously about ceremonies for your child before God. Avoid un-Biblical child/infant baptism altogether. There is no eternal benefit before God from the practice and it creates many problems for the future, such as what the child will be confronted with when they do decide for themselves to follow Jesus. Why rob them of the precious opportunity of true baptism in their own lives with Jesus?

Also think carefully about your choice of godparents. Consider the consequences of what you implicitly expect a chosen godparent, who may not be saved, to agree to through the words of the promise they will make before God and the church. This may place a great burden of eternal consequence on them. The decision is not to be taken lightly – we are calling the Almighty God as witness to that promise.

If you were to choose a godparent who may not be a true believer, explain to them the consequences of making a promise before God. If they can't do so in good conscience, then do not include them in that element of the actual ceremony. Instead ask them to be a godparent in a secular sense. While this does nothing for the child's eternity, it will honour God more than a knowingly false promise.

Repent of Unworthy Water Baptism

I believe church leaders and members must consider whether they must repent before God regarding baptism:

- Let those who were baptised as professing believers but didn't continue to follow Jesus in earnest and faith, meditate before God on their culpability before Him. Their lives may do great harm to the name of God.
- Let those who baptised infants in ignorance and realised afterwards the true place of water baptism, repent before God. Ensure the children you have baptised hear the truth about the reason and significance of baptism before God.
- Let those who were confirmed rather than baptised at their serious decision to follow Jesus, be baptised.
- Let those who refuse baptism while claiming a saving relationship with Christ repent of their disobedience.
- Let leaders of churches where infant water baptism and confirmation are used as alternative to believers' baptism, repent and change their ways, even if at their significant personal cost in the earthly church from which they derive their position. Can we knowingly officiate over un-Biblical

practices and false declarations before Almighty God to satisfy a worldly church system, and not think God will demand a reckoning from us? Then we too will fall foul of **_John 12:42_** *'Yet at the same time many even among the leaders believed in Him. But because of the Pharisees they would not openly acknowledge their faith for fear they would be put out of the synagogue'.*

Conclusion

Baptism is such an integral part of our journey of faith in Jesus. Let us come to Him with joy and be baptised in loving obedience, break with the old life, die to ourselves, believe in Him as our only hope. And let us enter into a joyful, permanent and public association with Jesus for the rest of our days.

8 Enter in: Find Jesus, Receive the Spirit

Volumes have been written about the Holy Spirit. In this chapter we will limit our discussion to the Spirit's rebirth and His validation of salvation. It brings together several points that have been discussed before. There will also be references to manifestations that may or may not be evident in you or your church. Please do not assume their presence or absence is God's silent approval; rather assess your own position before God based on all of Scripture.

People ask how to know if they are 'saved'. The short answer is: God confirms it to the believer by His Spirit. The Spirit is the only true mark of salvation, because that is what rebirth is – the Spirit of God puts His new life into us by taking up residence in us. He gives us the internal proof (*'The Spirit Himself testifies with our spirit that we are God's children'* **Rom 8:16**). When we enter through the gate of Jesus, we always receive His Spirit. Jesus says *'I am the gate; whoever enters through Me will be saved'* (**John 10:9**).

The Greatest Event

Being reborn of God is the greatest event for any human being. To become a child of the Living God by the Spirit is an unimaginable gift of grace. We move from the devil as our father to the Almighty God as our Father, from enemies of God to disciples, friends, brothers and sisters of Jesus Christ.

Take a moment to imagine the scale of the change. The God of the universe gave His Son to die so we can become a part of His eternal family, not because we deserve this, but in spite of our sinfulness and rebellion. We actually deserve the opposite! Salvation comes because of His grace, not our goodness. Even doing exactly what He requires, doesn't gain any 'spiritual brownie points' (***Luke 17:10***). I deserve hell no less once I stop my favourite sins than before! It is only God's grace that moves me from condemned to a child of His.

In many churches there are few new members joining the church as a result of evangelism. They are generally satisfied within their own ranks. People are born into the church, baptised as infants, confirmed, and the cycle repeats. This is deadly religion! Once in a while someone within the church family may actually be truly reborn of God, yet few understand what happened because they never received salvation themselves. They can't grasp that God demands and offers a relationship fundamentally different to what their have!

So many don't want Jesus to mess up their lives

In other churches we may be glad when we've converted another soul. We celebrate it with handshakes, cakes and tea and a Bible from the church, yet it may be a non-event in heaven. They added Jesus to their lives, but hadn't been renewed by the Spirit and their souls saved.

A true rebirth should be a great celebration, recognising the huge significance of the change!

Know for certain: God is galled at our human Christian traditions and innovations that demote Him to the back seat.

Infant christenings, confirmation ceremonies officiated over by the church officialdom, public figures coming to open new churches, fruit of the Spirit 'fruit tossing', meaningless and false Christmas carols sung on repeat, with words perpetuating falsehoods such as *'little Lord Jesus no crying He makes'*, and many more. None of this belongs in the body of Christ! Is it any wonder that the Spirit is absent from our churches? I confess was a part of it for such a long time!

Becoming a child of the Living God is the greatest event. *'Only a Few find it'*.

Rebirth is Always by the Spirit

Something went terribly wrong in the church movement that we ended up believing in salvation without the definite Spirit. Large swathes of the worldwide Protestant church (regardless of denomination, persuasion, formality, size), Catholic and wider ended up persuaded that salvation is assumed rather than confirmed by God. We determine when someone is 'saved'. This is deadly! God authenticates true rebirth by His Spirit. He is the Distinguishing Element.

Sadly, of the churches that do believe in the Spirit's rebirth, many stray into devilish manifestations. They know to expect certain marks of the Spirit's baptism, yet because rebirth wasn't real they assume the Spirit comes by human intervention! Only God gives what is only His to give.

Go to virtually any outreach, formal programme or even personal evangelism and observe what is being taught and what is assumed. You pray a sincere prayer or 'accept Jesus as your personal Saviour' or similar and you are 'in'! Listen with fresh ears to the questions of seekers once they have committed. We just declared over them that they are saved. Seekers often ask 'Is that it? Is that all I must do?' They are as astonished as God that it is 'so easy'! After the prayer, parroted after the speaker, they say they don't feel any different. Most evangelists then say salvation is a matter of fact – once you prayed the prayer you accept your salvation by faith: you are reborn! And those born into religious church families either assume they are automatically 'in' because they already 'believe in Jesus' and were baptised or because they made some form of commitment, even in early childhood.

Let us reconsider what we are intimating: people just made the greatest commitment and declaration of loving submission to the Son of God. They are told they just received the greatest gift to mankind: pardon for their sins, salvation, union with Jesus and eternal life. And yet someone had to lead them in a parrot fashion declaration to their new First Love! Is that how we deal with our greatest human love – ask someone else to speak the words we should say to our greatest love, so that we can just repeat it after them? How does the one feel who receives such an empty 'love declaration'? They prayed their prayer and are rebirthed by the very Spirit of God, set free from hell and now heaven-bound, yet they feel no different!

Does anything sound wrong to you yet?

This situation is then perpetuated: new 'born-again Christians' are swept up into church life. Baptism (and/or confirmation) further confirms their belief they are saved and some will go on to discipleship programmes. The church says they have received the Spirit, an assumed silent reception, the moment they said 'yes', when they 'received Jesus into their heart'. Thereafter they replicate to others what they were told themselves. They become even more convinced that this is salvation because they must often defend to others the very same doubts they had, thereby cementing the falsehood into their own minds.

Our churches are full of professing believers who went through this kind of evangelism and teaching. Once in the church for a while the last thing people want to hear is that their faith is deficient. Rather than find out the truth, they defend to the hilt the faith they profess. Many are sincere and committed, but God is not after our sincerity. All in or nothing!

So, where did we end up? With a faith where the Spirit of the Almighty God enters the believer at their commitment, yet nothing to confirm of this wondrous rebirth happened! Faith in Jesus now becomes faith that my faith saves.

We must ask ourselves: Would God allow this most important event in His child's life to go unmarked and unnoticed, with just a memory of what we did? Read **_1 John 3:24_** '*... And this is how we know that He lives in us: We know it by the Spirit He gave us.*' There are many similar passages. To <u>know</u> implies certainty, based on something definite and concrete, something evidential and memorable. Yet the church argues we are to believe it happened, that certainty is not personal experience but comes from assuming that what is in the Bible, is mine when I just believe.

Is everyone who assumes they are saved by believing, reborn? According to Jesus, NO!

What if I assume wrongly I am saved? Surely God should tell us plainly. And He does! We will return to this again later.

<u>Fallacy of an 'Assumed Spirit'</u>

God established the church in Acts by His Spirit; the Spirit entered every true believer. Those of the Spirit <u>are</u> the true church of Christ. Many claim the Spirit enters a believer automatically and that their action makes them a part of the church. The church 'houses' the Spirit, so they 'acquire' the Spirit by their decision.

There are major shortcomings with this assumption:

Firstly, the Bible talks about believing in Jesus and receiving the Spirit as two separate elements of saving faith. We don't receive the Spirit when we verbally combine 'believe' with 'receive' into one – 'receive Jesus'. (There is a single reference to 'receiving Christ' in **Colossians 2:6** but it refers to receiving the Spirit of Christ through God.)

Receiving the Spirit is a passive sense; God actively gives the Spirit, and we receive. We do not take hold of or claim the Spirit. This is evident from **Colossians 2:10-13** *'and in Christ you have been brought to fullness'* and (v11) *'you were also circumcised (of the heart)'* and (v12) *'having been buried'* and (v12)*'you were raised with Him through your faith in the working of God'* and (v13) *'God made you alive'*. We do not receive the Spirit by our own decision or assumption, but by God's sovereign grace. His decision is His sovereign mercy and based on His perfect knowledge of our First Love for Christ and faith in Him. We can't believe unto salvation from ourselves, and therefore receive the Spirit 'on demand'.

Secondly, who is the church? The church is the body of true Spirit-filled believers in Christ.

The earthly church is not a perpetual central body which houses the Spirit whom we gain when we attach ourselves by our decision. Many make the Spirit into a club membership facility: you join the church by praying the prayer and gain the Spirit. No, we either are church or we are not church. Individual believers make up the church. The Spirit is in the church only because He is present individually.

This may sound like an unnecessary repetition but it is core to saving faith and it is a crucial misunderstanding of what salvation is. The lifeblood of the Spirit, newly gifted to me, grafts me alive into the rest of the body, which also already has the life of the Spirit. I am not sewn onto the body a lifeless arm, after which a valve is opened and the blood is directed to my veins so that I also become a live member of the church. <u>To be a part of the body I must have received the Spirit already.</u> I don't share unless I am a constituent part!

There is no automatic, silent impartation of the Spirit when we decide we believe. We are only individually gifted the Spirit by God's grace at rebirth

---

Ephesians 1:13-14 reads *'And you also were included in Christ when you heard the message of truth, the gospel of your salvation. When you believed, you were marked in Him with a seal, the promised Holy Spirit, who is a deposit guaranteeing our inheritance until the redemption of those who are God's possession—to the praise of His glory.'* Faith, which God approves, is His gift and He authenticates it with the Spirit (*'For it is by grace you have been saved, through faith – and this is not from yourselves, it is the gift of God'* **Eph 2:8**). My faith is essential but my best efforts, even my strongest faith, changes nothing – I remain a guilty sinner – until I receive God's gracious gift of forgiveness and salvation. Over this gift He decides sovereignly.

When Paul met the twelve Ephesian disciples, he asked *'Did you receive the Holy Spirit when you believed?'* (**Acts 19:2**). Why ask? Because the Spirit is God's mark that He accepted their heart-level change and validated them as true spiritual family. God led Paul to lay hands on them and they received the Spirit (*'God, <u>who knows the heart</u>, showed that <u>He accepted them</u> by giving the Holy Spirit to them, just as He did to us'* **Acts 15:8**). It was not their confession of faith ('*when you* [said or decided you would] *believed*') that made them brothers and sisters, but God's Spirit that gave and confirmed their identity.

In the case of Cornelius and his household, God confirmed their salvation by giving the Spirit first. Peter then knew he could not withhold water baptism from them as God already confirmed their acceptance by His Spirit. **_Acts 10:46-48_** reads *'For they heard them speaking in tongues and praising God. Then Peter said, "Surely no one can stand in the way of their being baptized with water. <u>They have received the Holy Spirit</u> just as we have." So he ordered that they be baptized in the name of Jesus Christ.'*

Thirdly, we do not become a part of the church or gain access to the Spirit gradually. God does not move in over weeks, months or years. The preparation may happen slowly and over years, but then it is an ON/OFF switch over which God has full control. We believe, love, obey, commit and give up. When God sovereignly decides to gift His grace, He changes the switch. He forgives. He gives the righteousness of Christ. He changes our nature by giving us His Spirit. And at that point we ARE church - the light is on! Our functions differ, but we are all live parts of one body - the body of Christ!

Study **_1 Corinthians 12:12-26_** for the link between the Spirit, the church as a body and us as members of that body. *'For we were all baptized by one Spirit so as <u>to form one body</u>.'* (**_1 Cor 12:13_**). The Greek word *'pas'* translated as *'all'* means <u>a whole picture, coming together one piece at a time</u>. We are <u>all baptised into the one body</u> by the same Spirit. <u>Spirit baptism makes us one body</u>; without Spirit baptism we are not part of the body of Christ! <u>Each one is individually gifted the Spirit</u>, one at a time. This Commonality makes us one body.

Holy Spirit – The Proof and The Truth

A human being cannot love Jesus to the Father's satisfaction, only the Holy Spirit loves Jesus as the Father requires. He enables us with true *agape* love for Christ. Without the Spirit we can at best admire, respect and revere Jesus or love Him like a first-choice brother (*phileo* love). He comes when we meet Jesus at rebirth and They (the Godhead) make Their home with us. Without *agape* love there is no salvation.

Every religion, including Christianity, claims to know God, yet only the Spirit validates true faith and salvation. Without the Spirit we are only part of Christian religion.

<u>Summary Truths of the Spirit and Our Faith</u>

- The Spirit came (was poured out) on the early church in a single advent. The special manifestations (sound of a mighty rushing wind, tongues of fire and miraculous speaking in actual and understandable languages the disciples never learned themselves) and miracles were powerful proof to others that this 'movement' was of God. The Spirit was also the proof to other believers of the spiritual status of others. And the Spirit confirmed the inclusion of Gentiles in salvation. '*Did you receive the Spirit when you believed?*' (**Acts 19:2**) became the password of the early church. The Spirit distinguished true faith from deficient faith then, and He still does now.

- The Spirit distinguishes the One True God from every other god of every other religion.

- The Spirit birth is like human birth – it happens once. He confirms us as God's family, enables personal holiness and empowers our God-ordained ministry.

- Can we be filled by the Spirit afterwards again? Yes, Paul encouraged us to keep ourselves 'topped up' all the time (***Eph 5:18***). Yet that is not rebirth.

- What about those who experienced the leading of the Spirit, in significant ways, even a lifetime of ministry, but without the definite receipt of the Spirit? That is the Spirit with us, not the Spirit in us. God does not leave us alone to find Him on our own until we are reborn. He leads, guides, encourages and proves His existence to us. During this time He will use us as He sees fit. He points out the truth by the Word, by healings, by answers to prayer. He shows us He can be trusted with our total lives and gives us every proof and every reason to believe in Jesus and to believe His words. As we discussed in Book 1, being used by God should not be confused with salvation. A lifetime of ministry may come to nothing. [*Even the likes of Martin Luther, John Wesley and many more only received the Spirit (i.e. were saved) many years into active service, Martin Luther well after he hammered his 95 Theses to the door, John Wesley years after he was already in active service in mission.*]

The True Church

What is the definition of the true spiritual church, the Bride of Christ? It is the company of those who are in a living fellowship with Jesus Christ and share the Spirit with Him.

The true church of Christ is a small group of possessors amongst a large group of confessors. Their existence is divisive amongst all the world's religions and even within Christianity. Why? Because of Who they belong to. Of them Jesus said *'Do not suppose that I have come to bring peace to the earth. I did not come to bring peace, but a sword'* (***Mat 10:34***)' and *'If* *the world hates you, keep in mind that it hated Me first. If you belonged to the world, it would love you as its own. As it is, you do not belong to the world, but I have chosen you out of the world. That is why the world hates you. Remember what I told you: 'A servant is not greater than his master.' If they persecuted Me, they will persecute you also'* (**John 15:18-20**).

The Spirit is the core difference between the true church and every other human in the world. The 'world' is not just those of no religion or of all other religions, but also the Many, even sincerely devoted religious, within Christianity. We are either rebirthed of God or remain of the world (of the devil).

There are no 'people of God' that aren't reborn by the Spirit

---

Spirit-filled believers live lives that can only be explained by the Spirit. To others their lives seem radical and senseless.

Are All Believers Saved?

This is an important question. From our discussions so far, 'believing in Jesus' is the short form reference to all truths that make up 'every effort' to enter. It is not a shortcut to salvation. True faith in Christ demands that all elements are present.

So, are all believers saved? The answer should be 'Yes'. But sadly, in the church context the answer is 'Absolutely Not!' How is that possible? It is because of how we define a believer, rather than God's definition. On the other hand, all believers by God's definition, i.e. a much smaller group and all marked by His Spirit are saved.

Can I Be A Follower (Disciple) Yet Be Unsaved?

As with the previous question, yes, I can be a disciple and be unsaved. My salvation does not come because I decide to follow. Many may decide to follow but not take Jesus seriously. They are followers of the faith, but not 'His disciples'. In His time, many disciples took issue with His words and the cost of following and walked away physically. *'From this time many of His disciples turned back and no longer followed Him'* (***John 6:66***). In our era some leave the church; others remain in the church yet 'unfollow' Jesus in passive resistance or find another church that preaches the message they want to hear.

The Significance of the Rebirthing Event

Spiritual rebirth brings the greatest differentiator between people: those belonging to God against those belonging to the devil (we don't belong to ourselves; it's either God or the devil). There is no greater honour than to be filled with God's Spirit. Old Testament characters marvelled at the future when this would happen (e.g. the outpouring and indwelling of the Spirit prophesied in ***Ezekiel 36:24-29*** and ***Joel 2:28-32*** [quoted by Peter in ***Acts 2:16-18***]).

It is difficult to express the true scale of the Spirit birth.

Firstly, understand something of the Source of Salvation. Our understanding is so limited because the earthly life is all we know: its ups and downs, its momentary joys and tears, its tiny scope in terms of location, impact and time. Our lives are just the wink of an eye in terms of the duration of creation. Yet, compared with the unfathomable scope and duration of eternity, this world's duration is negligible. Eternity is beyond our capacity and sanity level. And yet, eternity cannot begin to compare with the scale of Christ, the Creator. He dwarfs the indescribable intricacy, complexity and scope of creation and of eternity itself. This unfathomable Christ died for mine and your sins. This is seismic and beyond us.

Secondly, there is our spiritual rebirth. In terms of scale, it diminishes all else in our earthly lives by several orders of magnitude. Neither your wedding day nor those of your children, nor the birth of children or grandchildren, neither being freed of cancer, nor the loss of life or limb of a loved one, nor the achievement of a lifelong dream, nothing can ever compare. By the mercy and grace of God He takes us from eternal death to eternal life. And He comes to live in us!

Let's imagine a human event of great earthly proportions: Imagine a poor commoner gets engaged to marry into a rich royal family. The future bride is carefully chosen; one who truly loves the prince, not just one who is drawn by the glamour and riches of the palace. There is an engagement day and a ring as proof of the promise to marry. There is a change in status – the person is now known as the fiancée of the prince. The couple themselves are very aware of the change, as are everyone else inside and outside the palace. The newcomer begins to share in some privileges and full access will be granted on the wedding day. Before the engagement there was an exclusive relationship between the couple, but this becomes 'sacred' at engagement. They have daily contact and great expectations for the wedding day and for the life after. They do things together to prepare for the wedding day and their real purpose is their lives together after the wedding.

How does this compare in eternal terms? Before He gives His Spirit the Father only chooses the future Bride who loves Jesus more than anything - an exclusive 'First Love' relationship. He chooses someone who isn't after the benefits of heaven, but only sees His Son. **_Isaiah 53:2_** said *'He had no beauty or majesty to attract us to Him, nothing in His appearance that we should desire Him'*. He wants someone who only wants *'to gaze upon His* [inner] *beauty'* (**Ps 29:4**). They must want His Son forever. The great prize is to be with Him; the rest is incidental. The King will weed out the spiritual 'gold diggers' who just want the benefits of heaven (and earth).

So, if God wishes to do this greatest miracle work in the life of His newly adopted child, would He not want it to be memorable, with clear proof? Or would He hide it from them and so they doubt they are in His family? Must they rely on hearsay and on others to convince them that they are 'engaged' to Jesus, or would He tell them clearly? Would He want them to remember this time in their lives? The answer is obvious.

God attaches so much value to the rescue of His created beings that He does not want His chosen ones to doubt

---

God gave His Son in the costliest purchase; therefore He ensures we know for certain. Spiritual birth is clear, on a day, memorable, no ambiguity. This isn't self-assurance, self-illusion or assumption. The core qualities of saving faith are surety and certainty and we obtain that only from God. Every evidence in Scripture is that New Testament believers were fully aware of the event. This is still the case.

Paul writes *'Therefore, if anyone is in Christ, the new creation has come: The old has gone, the new is here!'* (**2 Cor 5:17**). The old has gone – the damnation, the old life, the old doubts. Now that the old has died, the old wilful sins won't continue unchecked. The glorious new has come. The Spirit now lives in me. Past sins and desires of worldliness, however well disguised, were the evidence the old life was still alive. The new works of the Spirit show the new life has come.

Many Are Called, Few Are <u>Chosen</u>

'Many are called but few <u>are chosen</u>' (**_Mat 22:14_**). <u>God chooses</u>; we do not self-select. In His mercy God calls many. 'He is patient with you, not wanting anyone to perish, but everyone to come to repentance' (**_2 Pet 3:9_**). He knows we are dust (**_Ps 103:14_**) and gives us every help and chance to find Jesus, but He won't lower His standard. Rather than seek the Son, most people just want heaven or escape hell. They are not in awe of Jesus at all. They want a guarantee and then continue living as they did before – for themselves. Heaven is an extension of their selfish life of the earth.

The Father is the gatekeeper/watchman (**_John 10:3_**). He chooses the sheep for the Good Shepherd (**_John 10:29_**). God makes a great deal of His new children: He helps them overcome and gives them His seal of the Spirit as a reminder and guarantee of what is to come and uses them in His work.

What about the Many who have not been chosen? Will the Father be happy if they try to select themselves? If they falsify the seal ring and claim to be a part of His family? That is what the Many do. Perhaps unwittingly, but still!

God keeps calling because He does not want any to go lost. The Many claim to be part of His Royal Family. They believe saying 'yes' takes them from the line-up to the palace, but it doesn't. God must say 'Yes'. When they come for their inheritance they will hear 'you were never mine'.

Some are deeply sincere, great Bible students, ethical and living by strict Christian discipline. They may do everything in the church, for a lifetime, yet hang on to things they value more than Christ. Their situation will be the saddest. Just outside the narrow gate but never entered.

God does not perform powerless still-births

Many say they are 'not perfect', but it never occurs to them they are actually lost, just like those outside the church. It's very likely their churches don't teach the full counsel of God, nor do they study the Word of God for themselves. Or perhaps they haven't been awakened to the truth of God yet.

Can you imagine how many in our churches are in this condition? Christians for many years, committed to the church, yet satisfied to be religious?

If you're in doubt about where you stand, get alone with God. Don't stop until you are absolutely certain. But be prepared, it's hard to realise you aren't saved when you thought you were.

How to Receive the Spirit

This is a crucial question, yet the answer is quite short and may be very different to what you expect!

We are instrumental in preparing our hearts for rebirth, but we are not instrumental in receiving rebirth by the Spirit. The Spirit is God's gift of grace. Jesus encourages us to ask the Father for the Spirit '... *how much more will your Father in heaven give the Holy Spirit to those who ask Him!*' (**Luke 11:13**). We don't wear God down until He gives in; we ask God for the Spirit, and He will call us to draw near. As we remain at His feet, He will show us why He is not yet able to give us the Spirit – sin, disobedience, legalism, other loves, etc. We don't receive just because we ask but because our hearts yearn for Christ. The Father gifts us the Spirit when He decides (**Gal 3:2** '... *Did you receive the Spirit* ...?' **Gal 3:5** '... *does*

God give you His Spirit ...' **Gal 3:15** '*... that by faith we might receive the promise of the Spirit*').

We don't receive the Spirit at a specific church or event or from an 'anointed leader'. One human cannot give or affect the Spirit baptism of another. It is merely incidental if God enacts the event through the prayer and/or the laying on of hands of someone else. In **Acts 19:2** Paul laid his hands on the 12 disciples in Ephesus and they received the Spirit. Because of Paul's actions? No. God gave the Spirit because He chose them. In this case God used Paul as the 'vehicle' to enact the event.

Receiving the Spirit is not a mechanical process of people being told what to do to receive the 'gift', as with un-Biblical tongues, which is entirely man-induced. God acts sovereignly. If your past experience has been man-induced, then you must question whether you have received the Spirit at all.

You may be disappointed if you wanted a recipe to receive the Spirit and salvation, but '*Draw near to God, and He will draw near to you. Cleanse your hands, you sinners, and purify your hearts, you double-minded*' (**Jam 4:8**). We cast ourselves before God for His mercy, and we believe in Him for our salvation. We don't receive the Spirit because we want the Spirit; instead we are gifted the Spirit when God chooses us.

We don't work for our salvation; we empty our hands and plead on the basis of Jesus' righteousness

---

What Happens When I Receive the Spirit?

In this section we won't describe all elements of the incoming Spirit. Instead we will discuss why this is an unmissable event.

Receiving the Holy Spirit is unmistakeable and we are acutely aware. Regardless of whether you know exactly what happened spiritually, it will be memorable for all your life. You will look back on that period with a longing for the intense presence you experienced on the 'mountain top' with God.

The exact manifestation is the gift of God, perhaps in a way the receiver will remember most vividly or find most meaningful. Whatever happens, there is always *a verbal 'confirmation' of sorts.* For some it's a single shout (perhaps never repeated again) as they 'overflow' with joy. Some may speak in a different language ('tongues'). If so then it will be a definite language they never spoke before, whether single words or fluent speech, but not babble, and no-one will need to teach you how to speak either. (Be careful of those whose 'tongue' is 'an ancient language from the East'!) There will also be an immense sense of *peace* and the *presence of God,* an *intense sense of love* and *forgiveness.* Many are tearful. Some speak of such an overwhelming blessing that they even asked God to limit it because they were not able to deal with its intensity in their natural state.

As for gifts of the Spirit, some receive *prophetic* gifts, others for *healing,* for *teaching,* etc. Miraculous healings continue today and they result from God's sovereign power, not of the person praying, and certainly not commanding! We don't speak our desired outcome and command God to act (so-called 'speaking in faith' – i.e. using God to do what we want to have happen). Instead we await His inner 'instruction' <u>to us</u> to act on His command. This is what Jesus did. He made clear He did and said exactly <u>what He received from His Father</u>. We are to do no different!

The incoming Spirit also brings a *powerful witness,* a *conviction* and a *boldness* that was never there before, *power in ministry* and *power to overcome besetting sins,* etc. Before, someone may have struggled with witnessing, yet afterwards the Spirit enables our powerful, effective witness.

The infilling of the Spirit always manifests the fruit of the Spirit: *'love, joy, peace, patience, kindness, goodness, faithfulness, gentleness and self-control'* (**_Gal 5:22-23_**) and it will become increasingly evident in us. Some elements may take longer than others to develop, yet if any of these remain absent, we should question whether we received the Spirit.

There is *certainty in faith* (**_Heb 11:1_**). Meeting Jesus in person gives undeniable proof that is now 'owned'.

Most important is the Spirit brings a *deep sense of love* – truly sacrificial, God-induced *agape* love, and we're able to overcome the most disagreeable persons and conditions.

---

*Agape love is core to salvation (**1 Cor 13**). Without agape, that faith is deficient*

Agape is our love towards God, love towards the brothers and sisters in the faith, and love for our neighbour. Many Scriptures speak of this love, typically: **_1 John 4:7-8_** *'Dear friends, let us love one another, for love comes from God. Everyone who loves has been born of God and knows God. Whoever does not love does not know God, because God is love'* and **_1 John 4:21_** *'And this commandment we have from Him, that the one who loves God should love his brother also'*. Each instance (and **_1 Cor 13_**) uses *agape*.

GOD IS AGAPE. Therefore, wherever His Spirit is, there is agape love

---

Before we are filled with the Spirit we acted out of choice, obedience and compulsion. Afterwards, loving others is part of our spiritual DNA. We forgive out of love, because God has forgiven us. Nothing I must forgive comes close to His forgiveness. We give out of love, because our God provides. Out of love we choose to do good things for another, even at great cost to ourselves. God is not physically present; therefore our *agape* shows in our sacrificial *agape* for the children of God. *Agape* for one another is also the witness to others that we are disciples of Jesus (***John 13:35***).

If *agape* is absent, then God's Spirit is absent. Without that love we are a *'resounding gong or clanging cymbal'* (***1 Cor 13:1***). It is not the preferential treatment of others because we share a common belief. We are not in a gang – they help one another for selfish reasons – they want a sense of love, belonging and benefit. No, we are driven by love that comes from the Spirit and doesn't expect anything in return. We love even our enemies at great cost to ourselves, because Jesus is our Lord and example.

Jesus promises *'Where two or three of you are gathered there I will be also'* **Mat 18:20**). Does He need to be invited? No. He said He will be there. He will bless the us with greater gifts than for individuals on our own.

I am not a great fan of acronyms, but I once found this one (source unknown) which I amended. It summarises the realities of Spirit life quite accurately:

- **B** Boldness to proclaim the Good News.
- **A** Assurance of God's Fatherly *agape* and my salvation through Christ. Also of my *agape* for God and others.
- **P** Power to speak, witness, to heal, etc.
- **T** Tongues, real languages that are unknown to the speaker.
- **I** Inspiration, i.e. prophecy.
- **S** Serving as we are led and anointed.
- **M** Mission, to make disciples of all people groups.

Will I receive all gifts of the Spirit? Probably not. Receive all my gifts simultaneously? Probably not. I am filled with the Spirit and may receive the gift of prophecy for the benefit of the whole body of Christ, but not other gifts at that time. Yet later God may decide to also give me other gifts. Due to a lack of space we will not discuss the gifts of the Spirit here.

Find Jesus, Being Known by Christ

We return to one of the core passages for the message of this book, namely **Matthew 7:23**: *'Then I will tell them plainly, "I never knew you. Away from Me, you evildoers!'*

What is it to be known by Jesus? Essentially it is when we meet Jesus personally. The original Greek *ginóskō* means to know, through personal experience and with certainty. It is also used more intimately such as in **Luke 1:34** *'And Mary [a virgin] said to the angel, "How will this be since I do not know (sexual intimacy) a man?"'* To have a real relationship with Jesus Christ, He must know me intimately (*ginóskō* knowledge), like a relationship between a husband and wife. It is exclusive, deep and personal. It is interesting that Paul corrects himself in **Galatians 4:9** when he says *'But now that you know God – or rather are known by God.'*

It is more important that Jesus knows us than that we claim to know Him

---

Jesus' *ginóskō* knowledge certifies the authenticity of our relationship. We are sons and daughters because He placed His 'seed' or new life of the Spirit in us. Therefore, we are reborn, but not of Adam's seed but God's seed. That makes us legitimate children and heirs of His kingdom.

Jesus said in **John 10:14-15** *'I am the Good Shepherd; I <u>know</u> My sheep and My sheep <u>know</u> Me— just as the Father <u>knows</u> Me and I <u>know</u> the Father.'* Every instance of *'know'* uses *ginóskō*. Just as Jesus knows the Father intimately, so too will He know those who enter by His gate at a deep level. Jesus said in **John 10:27-28** *'My sheep listen to My voice; I <u>know</u> them, and they follow Me. I give them eternal life, and they shall never perish; no one will snatch them out of My hand.'* As a mother and baby in nature recognise one another amongst hordes of other animals, we know the voice of Jesus when He speaks spiritual truths to us, even in the clamour of conflicting and misleading voices around us.

'To the Jews who had believed Him, Jesus said, "If you hold to My teaching, you are really My disciples. Then you will <u>know</u> the truth, and the truth will set you free" (**John 8:31-32**). This passage appears amongst discussions about Jesus' divinity, which the Jewish leaders refused to accept. Some Jews believed, yet He insisted on their obedience too. Their obedience would show they submitted to His divinity <u>and</u> Lordship. Only then are they His disciples.

Do you remember our discussion on interpreting the Bible, and the use of the word '<u>if</u>'? Here it is again. They already believed in Him, but He must be Lord too. *'<u>If</u> you hold to My teaching ... <u>then</u> you will <u>know</u> the truth and the truth will set you free.'* Then they will <u>know</u> the truth. Conditional!

This intimate relationship has a starting point (at rebirth), it grows (living by faith in a relationship daily) and it attains (at the wedding banquet in heaven).

In **John 14:21** Jesus says *'Whoever has My commands and keeps them is the one who loves Me. The one who loves Me will be loved by My Father, and I too will love them and <u>show Myself to them</u>.'* Can I be saved without being 'known' by Jesus? No. The words of Jesus in **Matthew 7:23** are *'Away* *from Me you evildoers, I never <u>knew</u> you.*' We claim to know Him but He does not recognise our intimacy. Only a *ginóskō* relationship saves - me in Him and Him in me (**John 15:4**).

Once we are gifted this intimate knowledge of Jesus, **Galatians 2:20** becomes true for us '*I have been crucified with Christ and I no longer live, but Christ lives in me. The life I now live in the body, I live by faith in the Son of God, who loved me and gave Himself for me*' [NLT: '*My old self has been crucified with Christ*']. This leads into **John 17:21-23** '*that all of them may be one, Father, just as You are in Me and I am in You. May they also be in Us so that the world may believe that You have sent Me. I have given them the glory that You gave Me, that they may be one as We are one. I in them and You in Me*'.

What then of the joy some may feel when they heard Jesus died for them? Is that baptism in the Spirit? Let us consider the Parable of the Sower. Jesus said of the seeds that fell in the rocky soil '*they received the message with joy ... But when the time of trials came they fell away because they had no root*' (**Luke 8:13**). I can be elated when I hear Jesus died for my sins and experience an emotional moment. Yet without the Spirit there was no salvation. There was no depth, no root planted in the deep soil of Godly sorrow and repentance. To be glad that Jesus died for my sins has no value if I don't fully surrender to Him. I can fall away from true following even while I am active in the church, while I continue a prideful, sinful or selfish life. Such a life ultimately continues in sin and disobedience, even if I am convinced I am not!

Man-made Manifestations

This section may be particularly difficult and troubling for some very sincere, even long-standing believers. Please pray before you read this that God will shine His light of truth on it.

False assurance in a false salvation is worse than a lack of salvation assurance!

The Holy Spirit comes only in sovereign Biblical ways. He IS. Therefore, God decides and He acts independent of us. The Spirit is only given to those the Father chooses. We cannot decide to teach someone to 'pray in tongues', etc. (If someone is reborn already we can pray that they receive this gift too.)

We may start to follow closely and earnestly and believe in the facts about Jesus, yet we must also submit to Him (we cannot have the Saviour without the Lord). When we therefore assume we are saved but we don't have God's confirmation, it is only natural that there will be a yearning for a deeper spiritual experience to validate this faith.

Many try to fill this void themselves. Sadly the modern church assumes the Spirit and His manifestations come at their own or someone else's action (or claim) rather than God's sovereign gift and that it is a 'second blessing' after salvation rather than that the true Spirit is received at salvation itself.

Like the Baal prophets on the Mount Carmel who cut themselves to spur their idol god into action (***1 Kings 18***), those who were never reborn kindle their own 'strange fire' (refer to Nadab and Abihu in ***Leviticus 10:1***). They lay hands on one another and receive manifestations of a spirit that is not from God. They end up with the un-Biblical manifestations typical of the **Kundalini** spirit of Hinduism: babbling, falling backwards ('being laid down in the spirit'), animal behaviour, uncontrolled rocking, involuntary movements, 'drunkenness in the spirit', laughing uncontrollably ('holy laughter') and the like. This is a massive deception and/or a blatant worldly lust for spiritual manifestations rather than for Christ.

These falsehoods are often surrounded by the further dross of prosperity theology (promises and expectations of good health and easy prosperous living) which further increases worldliness in the church. If we can assume our own salvation and make our own spirit manifestations, then we can 'speak' our own prosperity! This opens unholy floodgates, and acceptance of every worldly value and other faiths in a 'loving spirit of inclusion' is one step behind.

If Jesus or the apostles did not do it or teach it, or if it did not happen in the Bible, then approach that great red light with extreme caution!

The Spirit of God is not in these manifestations. It must be called out for what it is: a demonic spirit. It originated as the 'Toronto Blessing' and it spread like wildfire throughout the Christian church through books, conferences, charismatic speakers, etc. It has decimated the modern church.

If you need proof that this is demonic then think of this: God is love and He is a God of order. He made man in His own image (**_Gen 1:27_**). Would this God ever demean the crowning glory of His creation by directing them to behave like senseless animals and uncontrolled lunatics <u>when His Own Holy Spirit comes to reside in them</u>?

Are we saying without the Spirit we acted like humans; then God enters us and we act like lunatics and animals?

These manifestations are NOT of God! How can anyone even begin to imagine that the HOLY God will choose to make His home with His most precious child, and intentionally bring upon them behaviour that reduces them to lunatics or to the animals He ordained for man to rule over! That, when God enters the believer's body, the temple of the Spirit, it turns into a madhouse? This madness is what these professing believers say the Holiest God looks like. As for uncontrolled behaviour, where is 'self-control' as a part of the fruit of the Spirit that they are supposed to have received?! And as for falling: in the Bible people fell before God either on their faces in fear, awe and worship or backwards in judgement (Eli in **_1 Samuel 4:18_**). Judge for yourself God's heart in this.

What blasphemy to associate any of these manifestations with the Holy God! This is not just a small error of judgement but to fundamentally ignore and twist the truth of Scripture! It is to associate the <u>HOLY</u> Spirit with behaviour unbecoming the <u>HOLY</u> God, to attribute behaviour to Him what is demonic. Is this not perhaps a modern blasphemy of the Spirit?!

For those caught up in these manifestations, please understand that God does not send manifestations at rebirth but He enters in as the Godhead. Our behaviour with the Spirit is therefore a direct reflection of the very nature, holiness and sovereignty of God. **_Isaiah 50:11_** (NKJV) gives a very clear warning from God on this: *'Look, all you who kindle a fire, <u>who encircle yourselves with sparks</u>: Walk in the light of your fire and in the sparks you have kindled — This you shall have from My hand: You shall lie down in torment'*. All these manifestations are indeed the 'sparks' of the unholy fire that people kindle for themselves. Let us take heed of God's warning: *'This you shall have from My hand: <u>You shall lie down in torment</u>'.*

If we won't embrace the God of the Universe and His ways, don't study His Word and want a spiritual show, then Satan will deceive us even deep in the church!

And once someone believes they are saved and their faith was 'validated' by this counterfeit spirit, the devil has inoculated them against the Truth almost permanently. This is deception on an unimaginable scale.

If these manifestations are demonic, can people, who manifest in this way be one with Christ and therefore saved? In **_1 Corinthians 6:19_** Paul writes *'Do you not know that your bodies are temples of the Holy Spirit, Who is in you, Whom you have received from God?'* The question that I would ask is: Does God share His children with demons? Would the Holiest God co-exist with what is evil? Think of the demon-possessed man in the region of the Gerasenes (**_Mark 5:1-20_**). Jesus drove out his demons, after which the man was in his right mind. Jesus instructed the man *'Go home to your own people and tell them how much the Lord has done for you, and how He has had mercy on you.'* God's mercy on the man was to rid him of the demons and set him free and God moves in. God and Satan are irreconcilable. God cannot and will not co-exist with demons!

What then of the countless leaders and well-meaning followers who manifest in these ways? Jesus says His sheep know His voice and follow Him. Perhaps they fell into this without much thought but still **_Romans 8:10_** is true of them: *'And if anyone does not have the Spirit of Christ, he does not belong to Christ.'*

If you are involved in a church where this stuff happens or may be caught up in it yourself, then stop! Pray that God will protect you and show this falsehood clearly to shock you out of this deception. <u>You may be sincere but been misled.</u> Be very careful about remaining in a church where this stuff happens. If anyone prays over you and feels the need to teach you to babble, to touch you (especially your stomach area) except laying a loving hand on you, or expects you or someone else to fall, especially when they have a 'catcher' behind, then flee! Permanently! Stand up; refuse to behave in a way unbecoming of the Most Holy God. If God wants to lay you down, you will go down on your face, whether you intended to or not!

Even Greater Deception

It is already a terrible predicament in the Christianity that such demonic 'Spirit' manifestations have entered, yet they cause even greater issues than self-deception within the church.

Given their widespread prevalence, it is further assumed that anyone who is similarly 'blessed' also 'received the Holy Spirit'. This means their 'version' of Christian (or other) faith has supposedly also been 'validated' by God. One can only presume the logic may be based loosely on the account of **_Acts 10:44-48_** when Peter recognised the Gentiles at the house of Cornelius were saved because they already received the Spirit, just like the Jewish believers, and were baptised as brothers and sisters. If the deceived therefore see others (who in the past were considered the mission field of the Christian church) receiving the same manifestations as the professing church, this is assumed as validation that they too are saved in Christ.

Nothing could be further from the truth! And yet, as a result of this falsehood, all manner of false believers and cults, and even other religions too, are considered 'brothers and sisters in the faith', thereby further contaminating Christian churches. And all this because professing Christians assumed their salvation on the strength of a prayer and claiming an entitlement to the Spirit. <u>It results from false and deficient teaching, however and wherever assimilated.</u>

Satan managed to deceive even the sincere with a false faith, a false spirit and a false sense of inclusion in salvation, causing a massive falling away from the truth of Christ! In an instant Satan shrank the mission field by several order sizes as he validated his own children as true believers at the centre of the church. They gladly received what Satan gladly gave them!

What deception! False conversions and manifestations make churches grow when they draw people in with an unholy heady concoction of the 'charismatic' and easy salvation. Few are deceived by openly satanic messages, but a false message, cloaked in Christian sincerity, is the deception of the age. The church is misled, confused and wrongly fear accusation of judging others (read **_1 Cor 5:12_** and **_1 John 4:1_** instead).

How is the local church impacted by false conversions? Let's find a parallel in the cuckoo bird: it lays its eggs in the nests of 'host' birds that hatch and raise their chicks. The real chicks starve due to the care needed by stronger and more abundant intruder chicks. In the same way the devil has placed an unholy counterfeit in the church. True seekers and believers are being starved because the church let a counterfeit into the fold. Since new spiritual life never occurred, the unholy lifestyles of the un-rebirthed live on, if not in plain sight, then privately or in the heart. They bring a heavy pastoral workload. Time and resources to pastor them paralyse the earthly church as it tries to care for those who are not HIS disciples.

These unsaved further divert the message of the church to tickle their ears and accommodate their worldliness (**_2 Tim 4:3_**). Ongoing sin is inconsistent with a Spirit-filled life (**_1_**

John 3:9), yet they continue in sinful ways. The church devises programmes for claiming freedom from besetting sins and follows secular techniques clothed in religious speak. Even after completing the programmes, they remain unrepentant and the mission of the church is being derailed by the devil.

Oh God, how did we become so deceived!

This is very serious. If you are caught up in this kind of church, or in <u>any</u> of these manifestations, repent and get out! Get on your knees before God and ask Him to show you the true Christ and Spirit. Don't fall for misleading statements like 'God is creative and therefore He does new things'.

Identity and Freedom in Christ

When we are saved, we are in Christ and He is in us. He IS our identity and our freedom ('*If the Son sets you free, you will be free indeed*' **John 8:36**). We do not need to seek, find or claim our identity in Christ. Our freedom and identity are gained when the Spirit enters us and the Spirit already testifies with our spirit that we are children of God (***Rom 8:16***).

Keep asking God to guide you in specific areas where you may still cling onto your worldly life. The Spirit reminds us of things we refuse to give up. Surrender! A Spirit-directed process to identify remaining sins and bondages may help speed up the process but be careful of courses. The setting must be Godly sorrow and deep repentance and a clear understanding that on-going sin will never lead to salvation.

If we are truly in Christ, it will be impossible to keep on sinning ('*No-one who lives in Him keeps on sinning. No-one who continues to sin has either seen Him or known Him*' ***1 John 3:6***). True believers will already have relinquished all for Jesus, obeying His commands and been filled with His Spirit, so there may be fewer sins to deal with than at the start of the journey. Professing Christians cannot be free or be certain of their identity in Christ.

Identity in Christ is fact for the Few, and fiction for all others. Freedom is given to true believers who received God's grace. To all others their freedom is mere positive confession.

Attempts to confess positively and repeatedly about my identity in Christ will not change my status. There are books, courses and speakers on our identity in Christ. Yet the Many can at best achieve what every secular person can – follow secular methods (couched in religious terms) and expect secular outcomes. They may deal with individual weaknesses, but their core sinful disposition remains unchanged because Christ never 'knew' them by His Spirit.

Without the Spirit, my identity and freedom in Christ are no more real than for the atheist

---

We return to our early example: salvation is not a contract, pre-signed by God, that only needs our signature. No, God proposes the contract and we sign it. Then He puts us through 'due diligence' before He will sign. He will not enter into this union until we choose Jesus above all. **_1 John 3:24_** reads: *'Those who obey His commands live in Him and He in them. And this is how we know that He lives in us: We know it by the Spirit He gave us.'* It is as clear as day if we will hear.

Rebirth Is Into a Future Promise

<u>Into an Inheritance</u>

1 Peter 1:3-9 *'Praise be to the God and Father of our Lord Jesus Christ! In His great mercy He has given us new birth into a living hope through the resurrection of Jesus Christ* *from the dead, and <u>into an inheritance</u> that can never perish, spoil or fade. <u>This inheritance is kept in heaven for you</u>, who through faith are shielded by God's power <u>until the coming of the salvation that is ready to be revealed in the last time</u>. In all this you greatly rejoice ... Though you have not seen Him, you love Him; and even though you do not see Him now, you believe in Him and are filled with an inexpressible and glorious joy, for you are receiving <u>the end result of your faith, the salvation of your souls.</u>'*

The true prize of rebirth is not in this life (we do receive a deposit of what is to come), but a future inheritance in heaven. We are already grafted into God's will and receive the 'first fruits' of heaven. This is God's promise to us: nothing will take us from His hands. Yet, in order to receive the inheritance, we must continue to walk with Jesus to the end, as passionately and diligently as we started out when we received the Spirit. In **_John 15_** Jesus says clearly that we must remain in Him for Him to remain in us. Likewise, in **_Revelation 2 and 3_** Jesus says in the letters to the seven churches that, as the future Bride of Christ, we must keep ourselves pure, keep Jesus as our First Love and remain on fire (not lukewarm) for Him.

There isn't the space to debate this here (we will touch on this in Chapter 11 'On the Narrow Road'), but many claim 'Once Saved, Always Saved' at their peril. God promises that nothing outside us will ever be able to take us from His hand (**_Rom 8:38-39_**). Yet our future inheritance is conditional – 'IF'! We must remain! *'But now He has reconciled you by Christ's physical body through death to present you holy in His sight, without blemish and free from accusation – **if** <u>you continue in your faith</u>, established and <u>firm</u>, and <u>do not move from the hope</u> held out in the gospel* (**_Col 1:22-23_**). Given that God only chooses those who truly seek and love His Son for His bride, why will He continue with those who wilfully leave Jesus' side (after they received His Spirit) to go off with another lover?! '**IF**'!

<u>The Spirit is a Deposit</u>

'Now it is God who makes both us and you stand firm in Christ. He <u>anointed</u> us, set His <u>seal of ownership</u> on us, and put His Spirit in our hearts as a <u>deposit</u>, <u>guaranteeing</u> what is to come' (**2 Cor 1:21-22**).

'And you also were included in Christ when you heard the message of truth, the gospel of your salvation. When you believed, you were <u>marked</u> in Him <u>with a seal</u>, the promised Holy Spirit, who is a <u>deposit</u> <u>guaranteeing</u> our inheritance <u>until the redemption</u> of those who are God's possession—to the praise of His glory' (**Eph 1:13-14**).

The Spirit is an anointing, a seal of God's ownership, a deposit and a guarantee. A deposit is a pledge, a down-payment that guarantees future completion; the final reality will be of the same kind and for the full value. The Spirit is our deposit of what we will receive in heaven, a foretaste and a fraction of the future, just as the engagement is a foretaste of the wedding to come. Paul quoted from Isaiah *'No eye has seen, no ear has heard, and no mind has imagined what God has prepared <u>for those who love Him</u>'* **1 Cor 2:9** NLT). What God has prepared for the elect will outstrip our Spirit-filled life, peace and joy on this earth in inconceivable ways.

'Sonship'

God is 'the' Father. And for the Few God is 'our' Father. There is a distinct difference between the two.

God 'the' Father is a reference to the Father as the Giver of Life, the Creator of all creation, of both the redeemed and the unredeemed.

God 'our' Father is when at rebirth 'the' Father becomes 'our' Father of the Few. He creates a new spiritual being, an adopted son or daughter of the Living God. There is now a new relationship and deep closeness between us and our Father.

Jesus prayed to His Father in the Garden of Gethsemane '*Abba! Father! All things are possible for You; remove this cup from Me; yet not what I will, but what You will*' (**Mark 14:36**). '*Abba*' is of Aramaic origin and it is the name a small child in the Middle East calls their father, even today. 'Daddy'. Jesus called on His Father on the basis of this most intimate and endearing relationship. When we are adopted by the Father, He becomes our '*Abba*' too. Paul speaks of this relationship in the following passages:

Romans 8:15 '*The Spirit you received does not make you slaves, so that you live in fear again; rather, the Spirit you received brought about your adoption to sonship. And by Him we cry, "Abba, Father"*'.

Galatians 4:5-7 '[*God sent His Son*] *to redeem those under the law, that we might receive adoption to sonship. Because you are His sons, God sent the Spirit of His Son into our hearts, the Spirit who calls out, "Abba, Father." So you are no longer a slave, but God's child; and since you are His child, God has made you also an heir.*'

Isn't that amazing? We don't fear the judgement of the Father anymore ('*There is no fear in love. But perfect love drives out fear, because fear has to do with punishment. The one who fears is not made perfect in love*' **1 John 4:18**) and we can speak to Him in the most humbly submissive yet intimately loving manner – 'Abba'. We have been redeemed. We are not a slave (like the Many who are only temporarily in the house) but a child and an heir to the heavenly kingdom forever (**John 8:35**). Only the Few have this privilege. The two passages quoted above also say everything about our identity in Christ! The Many remain slaves, never have this identity and will continue to claim it by positive confession.

God's family is limited to those of the Spirit. The Many are not welcome in heaven; they are imposters

Once we are reborn of the Spirit, we have everything in common with Jesus and with other true children of God, yet we have nothing spiritual in common with the Many, the Christian religion, any other or none. We are of Christ, not of the world. To know Jesus is not a religion. The Spirit is what distinguishes true believers from the religious Christian gathering. Everything outside of Him is false and counterfeit.

There is no spiritual unity without the Spirit. We can get together, love and encourage others, but there is only spiritual unity with other Spirit-filled believers

This unity is with individuals across the world, even if we never meet them. There is a unique, Godly bond between true sons and daughters that isn't anywhere else in the world.

Praying 'The Lord's Prayer' (also called 'The Christian Family Prayer') brings us to a conundrum: what are we to make of the start of the prayer: 'Our Father'? The danger is that we assume we have a common Father when we pray this prayer. This danger isn't in the prayer, but in our assumptions, and how we use it as a religious overcoat in religious spaces. Let us be careful with parroting the prayer in our churches.

The prayer originated when Jesus' own disciples asked Him to teach them to pray. Starting the prayer with '*Our Father*' was true for them. Jesus also said '*My mother and My brothers are all those who hear God's word and obey it*'

(***Luke 8:21***). In case it needs spelling out: if we don't have a Father in common with Jesus, then we are not of the same family. There's no close association with Jesus or the Father.

The Love of God

The love of God is as certain as God Himself (*'God is love'* ***1 John 4:8***) and its true meaning is beyond our understanding.

Many evangelists tell people of the love of God almost as their opening bid. Yet the Bible never leads with God's love to the unrepentant. Bible verses about God's love were always spoken by those who already experienced His love. Even ***John 3:16*** was written to encourage those who believed already. Only they can vouch for God's love and marvel *'God so loved the world'*. How can they attest to this love? They experienced it first hand when their eyes were opened by the Spirit.

We Must Make Use Of God's Love!

God's love extends to all people, yet His love is only relevant to those who make use of it, chosen and sealed by the Spirit. What is the point of God's great love gift if we don't make us of it and be saved? God's love is meaningless unless we do, because there is only one purpose for His love – to be one with Him.

The 'Unconditional Love of God'

Some churches speak easily of the 'unconditional love of God', a phrase that isn't found in Scripture. The way it is presented makes God almost into the beggar, along with the out-of-context use of ***Revelation 3:20*** *'Here I am! I stand at the door and knock. If anyone hears My voice and opens the door, I will come in and eat with that person, and they with Me'* (this passage was NOT spoken in the context of evangelism, but to the lukewarm existing church – it is God's alarm to call them back urgently).

God's love for the world is unconditional but it means something much different to what we make of it. It means Jesus died everyone's sins, regardless of what we did (even if we committed murder) or even if we accept Him as Saviour or not. Isn't it amazing that Jesus suffered, even when He already knew so few will love Him back? He knew the price He paid for many would 'come to nothing' and that so many would even become His active enemies, yet He still paid for everyone's sins. We will never die for someone who we know in advance will cast away our sacrifice with contempt, yet this is what Jesus did – for so many Jesus died 'in vain'. We would call it madness, but this is God's unconditional love!!

The unconditional nature of His love does not mean anything more than what is described above. And to make use of this love, we must love Him back. That is the gateway.

Does the requirement to love God back make His love conditional? No, God will not withdraw the price He paid for us. That is paid already. This is why John 3:16 says *'For God so loved the world that He gave'*. Past tense, unconditional love already shown, already paid. He put His 'love cards' on the table when He took the first step.

But also Yes, in the same sense as one-way love is not the with the foundation or nature of marriage. There must be First Love from our side too. Jesus said in **John 14:21** '... The one who loves Me will be loved by My Father, and I too will love them and show Myself to them.' This is God's conditional love for a successful marriage. The Father and Jesus will love those who love Jesus. Else we don't share in His redeeming love.

God's love expression is unconditional, yet for us to share in His love is conditional

---

Against this background, is it right to tell the unredeemed that God loves them unconditionally, when they have not repented? It is unwise as it can lead them to assume the exact opposite of what God requires. It won't bring them any nearer to God, because they'll misunderstand God's love. The unredeemed (the Many and the rest of the world) cannot share in God's love. They never experienced sorrow over their sinfulness and appreciated Jesus' sacrifice.

Yes, God loves the unredeemed very much. People who are sorrowful gain from hearing this. But the same can't be said of the proud, it doesn't break the hard crust of that heart. In fact, they are further hardened!

Let us not wilfully cast the precious pearls of God's love before those who don't understand it and will abuse it in their selfishness. Let us start where Jesus started – with repentance.

Even the Few Get It Wrong!

Up to this point we mentioned the misunderstanding of Many for assuming they are saved. Yet there is an entirely different issue that must be raised, as this perpetuates wrong teaching, even by the saved Few.

Consider this practical scenario: let's say someone 'gave their life to Jesus' and were told they are saved but were still lost. Their ministries and lives may expand but they struggle on without God's presence.

Then, after a deepening of their faith this person is actually reborn by God's grace and receives the Spirit. This brings a new predicament: although they are now reborn they continue under the false understanding that their initial decision was salvation. They believe the Spirit they received is a 'Second Blessing' to empower their ministry rather than that it was their actual salvation! Although they do now live the

Spirit-filled life they still don't understand what God required for salvation in the first instance.

This is dangerous, because even true, on-fire believers can and do perpetuate a deficient message. They tell others of the Spirit experience and encourage them to seek this baptism as a wonderful empowerment, yet assume it is a desirable extra rather than salvation itself. In their deficient understanding they may even be the very ones who encourage others to 'pray in tongues' etc when they should warn them that without the Spirit they remain lost!

We must address this serious situation amongst the Few. Let those who received the Spirit proclaim the Truth and not unwittingly perpetuate the lies of Satan! We will touch on this again in the chapter 'A Major Divide'.

The Power Of 'I Know!'

1 John 3:24 reads '... *And this is how we know that He lives in us: We know it by the Spirit He gave us.*' This verse says two things: there is certainty in the memory of the event of the Spirit and a certain assurance by the Spirit.

Firstly, the witness of the definite event of Spirit rebirth is memorable and clear – we know it happened. If not the date, then a clear memory. Beforehand we said 'I believe' by positive confession rather than inner conviction. Now there is certainty – 'I know' because I met with Jesus personally. Faith is no longer believing that Jesus exists, but the certain knowledge that Jesus IS. This is faith at the deepest level and is a gift from God. Rebirth is 'hard spiritual fact' and it changes us radically inside because God gives us clarity. He does not give assumed, imagined or self-generated rebirths.

Secondly, the Spirit keeps witnessing to our spirit and this brings certainty in the present and a sure hope for the future.

Even if we lose our assurance momentarily, we can call to mind the event, and we receive the Spirit's on-going testimony – a lift in our spirit as the Spirit encourages us.

This Spirit-supported inner knowledge stands apart from any self-generated faith. I know of people who are convinced of Jesus and that He paid for their sins. They even saw vividly their sins being nailed to the cross and it brought them much joy. Yet, their lives never changed because they never broke with the old life. They will eventually revert back to the old life because their faith lacks the substance of the Spirit.

The Crucial Question

Evangelists have the habit of asking people: if you die today, will you go to heaven or to hell? Or we may ask someone if they are sure they are going to heaven. Biblically speaking, though, the question is not what we think or believe. Our assessment can be very wrong. Think of what Jesus said to the Many – they certainly thought they were saved and expected to be let in.

The single most accurate question for all professing Christians that eliminates all personal bias regarding salvation is **'did you receive the Spirit when you believed?'** (**Acts 19:2**).

Did God validate the faith you profess in Jesus? This is the most important question to ask ourselves, our loved ones and other professing believers. The boundaries of the question should by now be clear: The True Spirit is sovereignly given, not assumed received, claimed or induced by some man-made action. This is the faith that we should disciple – small gate, narrow road, Spirit-filled.

1 John 3:24 *'Those who obey His commands live in Him and He in them. And this is how we <u>know</u> that He lives in us: We <u>know</u> it by the Spirit He gave us.'*

The earthly church makes this statement false. All of the early apostles could testify not only to the fact that they received the Spirit, but that the Spirit testified on-going to their spirit that they are children of God.

I ask again: <u>Did you receive God's Sovereign Spirit to validate your professed faith and rebirth you</u>? Do you grasp how important this question is?

In Closing

I add this account in closing, because we must understand we are not saved by our confession, even if we are following hard, or in ministry or leading churches. Some may spend a lifetime burning their lives away for their faith in God or in Jesus. Yet only God graciously chooses.

The poem below is from the daily readings resource *Streams in the Desert* by L.B. Cowman (Zondervan, 1977). The reading for 7th August that introduces the poem is so accurate of the truth of the Spirit. It relates how Christmas Evans, the Welsh preacher, was filled with the Spirit on a day. <u>He was already a well-known preacher and was evangelising others.</u> Yet he tells of how on a day God led him to a quiet place. He was gifted agony and brokenness before God over his sins. It led him to repentance. This was followed by a deep sense of God's forgiving love and he received the Holy Spirit.

Note that <u>he had been following for a long time, even passionately, as a Christian.</u> He was in active ministry. Then God gave him light. The final rebirthing happened within single hours. God saw His true heart and gifted him Godly sorrow and he repented, the deep soil in which true faith grows. Only now was he truly broken over his sins and felt God's forgiving love. Had he already been saved when he made a commitment to follow Jesus for the rest of his life, these things would have happened already. He was a sincere and hard-working disciple, but not yet HIS disciple. He was a professing Christian with a heart for God and active in ministry, but never reborn. But then came God's salvation and he was filled with the Spirit.

After this event his ministry bore great fruit and a revival broke out in Wales. Why? Because now it was God speaking through him and accomplishing His work through a broken, surrendered and loving believer, reborn of Christ Jesus!

Given the detail of the account, how can we argue that Evans was saved at confession of his faith and that the Spirit was merely a 'second blessing'? No it was salvation, but now on God's terms!

May you truly seek Jesus until you find Him!

Oh the Spirit filled life; is it thine, is it thine?
Is your soul wholly filled with the Spirit Divine?
As a child of the King, has He fallen on thee?
Does He reign in your soul, so that all men may see
The dear Saviour's blest image reflected in thee?

Has He swept through your soul like the waves of the sea?
Does the Spirit of God daily rest upon thee?
Does He sweeten your life, does He keep you from care?
Does He guide you and bless you in answer to prayer?
Is it joy to be led of the Lord ev'rywhere?

Is He near you each hour, does He stand at your side?
Does He gird you with strength, has He come to abide?

Does He give you to know that all things may be done
Through the grace and the power of the Crucified One?
Does He witness to you of the glorified Son?

Has He purified you with the fire from above?
Is He first in your thoughts, has He all of your love?
Is His service your choice, and is sacrifice sweet?
Is your doing His will both your drink and your meat?
Do you run at His bidding with glad eager feet?

Has He freed you from self and from all of your greed?
Do you hasten to comfort your brother in need?
As a soldier of Christ does your power endure?
Is your hope in the Lord everlasting and sure?
Are you patient and meek, are you tender and pure?

Oh, the Spirit-filled life may be thine, may be thine,
Ever in your soul Shechinah may shine;
It is yours to live with the tempests all stilled,
It is yours with the blest Holy Ghost to be filled;
It is yours, even yours, for your Lord has so willed.

9 Famous Christians

The purpose of this chapter is to explore further the reality of the Spirit baptism as the only witness of salvation. We are covering old ground but from a different perspective so as to put this beyond doubt. It is also fitting that this chapter follows on the account of Christmas Evans in the previous chapter.

The Experiences Of 'Famous Christians'

I have come across two excellent books detailing the experiences of famous Christians when they received the Spirit: *They Found The Secret* by V. Raymond Edman (Zondervan, 1984) and *Deeper Experiences Of Famous Christians* by James G. Lawson (Whitaker House, 1998). Each relates the stories of about 20 famous Christians and is well worth a read. The books include, amongst others, accounts of John Bunyan, Hudson Taylor, Amy Carmichael, Oswald Chambers, Andrew Murray, John Wesley, D.L. Moody and General Booth (Salvation Army). These famous Christians are, of course, not the only ones to have experienced this marvellous event. Thousands upon thousands through the ages can testify to the same. Some become widely known, others serve in obscurity. We only hear of the famous because their stories make headlines!

The discussion which follows in no way reflects on any of these great servants of God nor on these two excellent books, both of which I highly recommend. We will, however, focus on the basic premise behind the books, which I believe must be addressed in the light of our discussions.

Premise of the Books

The point of departure of both books resonates with what is taught in the majority of Christian circles. Both authors assumed these men and women were saved at confession of faith. Several years after they 'became Christians' and many already served extensively in ministry, they then began to follow and seek Jesus seriously and surrendered to Christ. Subsequently they received the baptism of the Holy Spirit and, amongst others, their ministries grew dramatically. Let us investigate this in the light of our discussions of 'Only a Few'.

Both books assumed the believers' early salvation, yet this wasn't confirmed by God (i.e. an assumed silent birth). Some were aware of an increasing closeness with God as they spent time in His presence, but not of a life-changing Spirit in them or of an event. Before being filled with the Spirit their message was powerless, some were fearful, doubtful and struggling with besetting sins and their ministries were largely non-fruit-bearing. Then they received the Spirit. They became bold, their message became powerful, they were freed from besetting sins. Their ministries took off and there was much fruit.

Each of these people recorded this memorable Holy Spirit event anywhere between two years and 20 years after their initial conversion. They may or may not have remembered their original decision date, yet the event of their Spirit baptism was indelibly etched in their minds.

Let us explore where the assumption of early salvation leads us with a range of questions regarding the faith journey:
1. If there could be light years' difference between the faith of two people, how can anyone know, themselves included, that they were saved at their initial decision?

2. When they first believed, did they have the Spirit at all? How did they know they had received the Spirit?

3. What was the function of the 'early-stage Spirit'? By their own admission they continued to be afraid, powerless, burdened and doubtful. Should they not have expected a great change? Did the Spirit fill them in half-measures?

4. Since the authors of the books assumed these famous ones were already 'saved' at confession, should we assume it makes no difference to God if they never received the 'subsequent' Spirit baptism? Did God intend it only as a preferred option for some?

5. Why would God limit this wonderful Gift to so few of His true children? Does He not desire or expect every precious believer to be powerful in witness and ministry?

6. If salvation was granted on professed faith in Jesus, on what basis would God then have granted the Spirit baptism to a select few afterwards? On commitment, hard work? On surrender and obedience? By grace but only reserved for a few in some ministries?

7. Most importantly, though, the Spirit is the Third Person of the Godhead, the Spirit of God. They received Him. The Spirit wasn't a manifestation but actual receipt of the Third Person. There is a big difference! The Spirit gives manifestations afterwards as He determines [***1 Cor 12:7-11***]. Why then would the Person of the Spirit be granted on a different basis than Jesus? Are we separating Jesus and the Spirit in two events, i.e. receive salvation in Christ at conversion, and the Spirit later on?

Based on our study thus far, their assumed salvation leads us into questionable territory! Salvation is always by the Spirit rather than an assumption, otherwise it is like being told by a university to grade your own papers for a medical degree. You take their word; you believe you qualify and self-certify your degree (assumed salvation). Years later you are hauled before the courts (Judgement Day) and charged with practicing without proper qualifications. It turns out your 'qualification' was never recognised by the Medical Board (Jesus), so you were never allowed to practice ('I never knew you') and you are found guilty.

Does this sound right? Is this what you expect of a righteous God? That He would leave those who He claims to love so deeply that His Son died for them, to guess whether they are saved, and then finds the vast majority guilty?

It is clear from Scripture that only FAITH in Jesus saves. The words 'believe', 'believers' and 'faith' in relation to salvation and a saved life (or not) appear around 400 times just in the New Testament. But is this ANY self-certified faith?

To summarise then: the premise of the books, as is the assumption in most of Christianity (incl. Evangelicalism), is that we are saved upon our decision and that this greatest event in the person's life is unconfirmed by God. We <u>claim</u> a promise of Scripture for ourselves, without a nod or a wink from God, just an assumption.

Rebirth, Spirit Baptism and 'Second Blessing'

Bringing this discussion back to the Many and the Few, what are we to make of the two events: the decision to follow and the baptism of the Spirit?

Let us examine this quote from *They Found The Secret* (1984, p14) which summarises the issue:

'The pattern of their [the famous Christians] *experiences is much the same. They had believed on the Saviour, yet they were burdened and bewildered, unfaithful and unfruitful, always yearning for a better way and never achieving <u>by their efforts</u> a better life. Then they came to a crisis of <u>utter</u>*

heart surrender to the Saviour, a meeting with Him in the innermost depths of their spirit: they found the Holy Spirit to be an unfailing fountain of life and refreshment. Thereafter life was never again the same, because in one way or another they had learned what the apostle Paul had testified: "I am crucified with Christ; nevertheless I live: yet not I, but Christ liveth in me; and the life which I now live in the flesh I live by the faith of the Son of God, who loved me, and gave Himself for me." New life had been exchanged for old' (emphases added).

Consider this quote in the light of Scripture and our discussions so far. Is what the author described not exactly what spiritual rebirth is? Before they received the Spirit, they were acting in their own strength and efforts, burdened, bewildered, unfaithful and unfruitful – is that not what we are as unredeemed followers without the Spirit? And that we are saved not when we believe in our own way, but when Jesus meets with us in the *'innermost depths of their spirit'* (*'and I too will love him and show Myself to him'* **John 14:21**). We can have growing earthly ministries (*'Lord, Lord, did we not prophecy in Your name, drive out evil spirit in Your name and perform many miracles?'*) yet not have the Spirit (*'evildoers, I never knew you!'* **Mat 7:22-23**).

Even more telling of the glaring problem is that the author spoke of the crisis of utter heart surrender and being crucified with Christ after they assumed their salvation. Yet Jesus said if we do not give up everything, we cannot be His disciples! It isn't something we decide after we are already saved, it's a **pre-condition** of being His disciples!

Galatians 2:20 quoted by the author speaks of being crucified with Christ, i.e. dying to self. It's the same message as **Luke 9:23-24** *'Then He said to them all: "Whoever wants to be My disciple must deny themselves and take up their*

<u>cross</u> *daily and follow Me. For whoever wants to save their life will lose it, but whoever loses their life for Me will save it*. Therefore, if we do not die to ourselves and are crucified with Christ (picking up our cross), we cannot be His disciple – a **pre-condition**. Note further Paul wrote *'I live by the faith of the Son of God'*. Live by faith – is that not 'believing in Jesus'?

The author also comments *'New life had been exchanged for old'*. Again, is that not rebirth (*'if anyone is in Christ, the new creation has come: The old has gone, the new is here!'* **2 Cor 5:17**)? In **Luke 17:33** Jesus says *'Whoever tries to keep their life will lose it, and whoever loses their life will preserve it'* – losing our lives and dying to self are central to gaining new life in Christ – a **pre-condition** for salvation.

The author is exactly right that the Spirit's baptism is the exchange of old for new, yet Biblically this isn't a freestanding blessing, but it <u>is</u> salvation. What else happens at rebirth if not this exchange?

<u>Assumed Salvation</u>

When these Christians 'believed' or 'gave their hearts to Jesus', full surrender and love for Jesus had not yet taken place, because they only surrendered fully later. They may have thought they did but God sees the innermost heart. They were sincere and hardworking, but they weren't <u>His</u> disciples yet.

<u>What these famous Christians had before their Spirit event is no different to what we find in the majority of our churches: dedicated lives but not surrendered lives!</u> A sincere decision to follow, but not rebirth. If they hadn't initially surrendered, hadn't died to themselves and didn't have joy and peace (fruit of the Spirit that they are assumed to have received at rebirth), how can we argue their first state was rebirth?

Like these famous Christians were, we too can live active, successful Christian lives, have large and growing churches and ministries, be well-known speakers, authors of best-selling Christian books, serve extensively, yet still be lost!

The entire world's churches or large denominations can agree we can be saved without Spirit baptism, yet we will all be wrong if God disagrees – and He does!

Professing Christians can be in a state of assumed salvation for many years, even permanently. If they are really serious, God will engineer a situation that will encourage their full surrender (like these famous Christians). Sadly, for most professing Christians this won't happen. Why? Because they are not that serious about Jesus. They want heaven but they don't want Jesus to upset their lives. They are satisfied with their religion. They never had Godly sorrow over their sins or so they never NEEDED a Saviour DESPERATELY!

These famous Christians started out sincere and diligent. Deep in their hearts they truly wanted Jesus and lived for Him. When God finally opened the door to them, life changed dramatically and permanently.

In the book *Deeper Experiences of Famous Christians* (1982, p8) the author spoke of this event as *'It is the baptism, filling, or gift of the Holy Spirit, and the experience resulting from being filled with the Spirit.'* Again, I would ask, what else happens at rebirth if not that Christ is birthed in us by His Spirit, so that our bodies become temples of the Holy Spirit?

'You Are Clean'

There is an issue that is bound to come up for some regarding salvation without the definite Spirit. Jesus said to Peter when washing the feet of His disciples in **John 13:10** *'Those who have had a bath need only to wash their feet; their whole body is clean. And you are clean, though not every one of you.'*

These words were spoken before the Holy Spirit was poured out. The disciples were saved already because of their faith in Jesus. Some say this proves all people (also in the Old Testament) were saved without a definite baptism of the Spirit, that the Spirit is purely an anointing (like when Saul prophesied in **_1 Samuel 10:10_**), and that we are saved and receive the impartation of the Spirit silently. Those who do subsequently receive the Spirit consider it desirable but optional.

Jesus said the disciples were already clean because He knew their hearts. In these unique cases at the change-over from the Old to the New Covenant the Spirit was poured out and the disciples received the Spirit which confirmed their salvation at Pentecost. Jesus said beforehand *'And I will ask the Father, and He will give you another Advocate ... you know Him, for He lives with you and will be in you'* (**_John 14:16-17_**). The Spirit lived with them at the time. He was later given to be in them. Since Pentecost, all who came to true faith under the New Covenant (including all Gentiles who never believed before) were filled by the Spirit (evidenced by Paul's question to the believers in Ephesus in **_Acts 19:2_** *'Did you receive the Holy Spirit when you believed?'*). This is the salvation of Christ. This was the pattern for the true church then and it will continue until Christ comes for His Bride.

The Spirit, Salvation and Being Used by God

The Spirit that filled believers in the early church still fills the Few now. The same power that rebirthed, strengthened and enabled the believers of the early church is still received at rebirth now. To make a case for true but weak believers, overcome with besetting sins and without a radical transformation, belies the power of God's Spirit. Otherwise we could not say with Paul *'Therefore, if anyone is in Christ, the* new creation <u>has come</u>: The old has gone, the new is here!' (**2 Cor 5:17**) when the old, weak, sinful person still lives on.

The 'new creation' is not imaginary; it is a profound change when the Spirit brings new spiritual life!

What then of believers who experienced answers to prayer and felt led and used by God, even in important ways, yet cannot witness to rebirth by the Spirit? Are they saved? God uses who He wills, whether we are reborn or not. He may use a rich person, saved or unsaved, to give to the needs of the poor in His flock. He may provide a word in season through an unsaved pastor or even through a complete atheist. That does not show God's approval of the giver or the speaker. God may use answers to prayer to draw us closer, which again does not show His approval of us. Instead it is His infinite loving mercy to give us every reason and opportunity to believe in Him. Therefore, on the evidence of being used by God and answers to prayers alone, the answer must be 'No', they are not saved.

Spiritual giftedness is not a good indicator of salvation

My own first memory of someone reaching me with the Gospel is still vivid in my mind (even the person's words!), yet to my knowledge that man is utterly lost himself. And I can also speak of God's abundant use of even atheists to move me forward in my own faith, and of God using me in the lives of many others in my previously lost state. Being used by God is not proof of the Spirit, nor is spiritual giftedness!

The 'Practical Agreement' In the Church

A final comment on the book *Deeper Experiences of Famous Christians*: The author makes a statement that perhaps shows the core of the issue under discussion: *'as there is practical agreement among evangelical Christians with regard to the way of salvation, so there is practical agreement among those who believe in a Christian experience deeper than conversion'* (1982, p8). This implies a form of understanding amongst Evangelicals (and most other churches, for that matter) that salvation happens at our decision rather than God's sovereign action, without the definite infilling of the Spirit. What's more, churches declare salvation over those who never receive the Spirit during their earthly lives and remain in a weak, powerless and overcome state. They teach that the Spirit baptism is non-essential but desirable and only a select few share in it. And so people go to hell in their millions, blessed by the church! Tragic beyond belief!!

There Is No Spirit 'Second Blessing'

Paul says: *'And you also were included in Christ when you heard the message of truth, the gospel of your salvation. When you believed, you were marked in Him with a seal, the promised Holy Spirit, who is a deposit guaranteeing our inheritance until the redemption of those who are God's possession—to the praise of His glory'* (**_Eph 1:13-14_**), and *'For we were all baptised by one Spirit into one body ... and we were all given the one Spirit to drink'* (**_1 Cor 12:13_**).

The baptism of the Spirit is therefore essential to be a part of the Body of Christ! It can't be read any differently!

Churches may have a *'practical agreement ... with regard to the way of salvation'*, even if unwritten. Yet this common understanding does seem to exist across the theological and church spectrum. This is evident through the teachings of churches, well-known outreach programs, discipleship programmes, books, courses and conferences. This teaching is Scripturally unsound and very dangerous, because it leaves countless people in the dark! The devil has deceived the church about what salvation is, and millions remain lost as a result.

The nature of salvation is the exclusive prerogative and domain of God! <u>We can only seek out God's truth and agree with Him.</u> If God indicates clearly, yet all the world agrees on a different measure, <u>then the entire world is wrong</u>!

So, the baptism of the Spirit is not a subsequent event to salvation. There is no minor mute Spirit when I decide to follow Jesus and a 'Second Blessing' of anointing for public ministry for a select few later on. A baby may be perfectly formed and birthed, but without breath it is sadly still-born and lifeless. We need the Spirit's life and breath to be born spiritually alive! And what of those who will not be used in a public ministry – will they just have to continue living in a weak and overcome state? Surely not! All of us receive the same Spirit of God at rebirth (even if God may give more spiritual gifts to some at a later stage).

'Only a Few' and the Spirit

What does all this mean in the light of 'Only a Few'? That preciously few can speak of a God-inspired, God-led, sovereign spiritual rebirth of the Spirit. Our lives only become eternally fruit-bearing <u>after</u> the Spirit. Once reborn, the redeemed are extensions of God's own hand and under the blessing of God's Spirit Himself. Most of these famous Christians testified they did no more work, but suddenly people fell in repentance before God.

From my own experience and that of others I met on the way, it is clear that we can follow Jesus for many years, even sincerely and diligently, even building up considerable local and wider ministries, yet still not be a son or daughter of God.

In light of 'Only a Few', the acid test is: The Spirit either came mightily on the believer and continues to testify in us, or He hasn't. **Romans 8:9** confirms: *'And if anyone does not have the Spirit of Christ, they do not belong to Christ.'* God does not leave us guessing.

One final comment: The title *They Found The Secret* is accurate in some ways. However, it is not a secret they found, but true salvation in Christ. It is not a secret as if it wasn't told to everyone, but is it indeed true that the Spirit-filled rebirth is the 'secret' of life, both in this world and in the next to come. **Matthew 6:6** refers to that secret life with God *'But you, when you pray, go into your room, and when you have shut your door, pray to your Father who is in the secret place; and your Father who sees in secret will reward you openly.'*

Jesus says 'Keep on seeking and you will find.' And He also says, 'only a few will find it'. Both of these statements are true, of course. But this can mean only one thing: if the promise is that everyone who seeks, finds, yet only a few find, then the missing link is seeking until we find. Make every effort. Only those who will not stop until they find, and seek in the right place and in God's manner, will find.

There are few indeed, because Jesus said so. The evidence of the small number of true Spirit rebirths in our churches bears that out. If the earthly life takes priority for us, then our seeking will be unfocussed and relaxed and it will predictably end up in not finding, even if we claim we have found.

May you indeed seek until you find.

10 When God Waits

Meeting Jesus is worth every price paid, every tear shed and every hour waited. He is the purpose of life. Humans want instant results, yet God will not be hurried. We don't receive rebirth in our own timescales and expectations.

God's Test

What if I believe I have given up, repented, laid down known sins, sought Jesus, fully committed in obedience, chose Him as my First Love and He still does not come?

He may be using me in all kinds of demonstrable ways, like the famous Christians we discussed before, yet I haven't received His Spirit. What if I have pleaded, even with tears, when I know I live sold out to Him, does it mean He will never save me, even though I gave my life to Him in every aspect?

The answer lies in four parts:

Firstly, to search the motivation of our heart. We abandon our lives because Jesus is worthy not come a commercial spirit: I abandon my life to Him because I want something.

Secondly, I may feel certain that I surrendered all, but God sees the depths of my heart. There may be something I will not hear. Let us keep listening for the still small voice of God.

Thirdly, God waits for us to be ready. He delays for His sovereign reasons; He purifies our faith. He steers us in the right direction and may call us back repeatedly. He will only put that Treasure in a ready heart and empty hands.

The path will be what God decides: short for some and long for others. We don't know His reasons. But once we decided to place our faith in Jesus and follow, it should make no difference to us what God decides regarding His path with us. We can trust Him fully. God already knew Joseph would be ruler in Egypt yet he had to wait 14 years from this to happen. David was anointed king yet he had to wait 15 years. Some famous Christians in Chapter 8 served intentionally and faithfully up to 20 years before God gifted His Spirit!

Let us follow, regardless, and let God be sovereignly God. He prepares us for what He has in mind. *'Therefore the Lord will wait, that He may be gracious to you; And therefore He will be exalted, that He may have mercy on you. For the Lord is a God of justice; Blessed are all those who wait for Him'* (**Is 30:18** NKJV). This is so true because this is God's way!

Lastly, once I decide to follow Jesus, what would be God's clearest test of my true motivation? When He waits! Is my pledge permanent or dependent on getting what I want?

Will I waver in the permanency of my choice? Does my commitment have an expiry date?

Do I think I <u>deserve</u> salvation because I gave up? Or do I realise I don't deserve anything? Every part of my faith is His grace. <u>I cannot make even one demand on God to save me, even if I do everything He says.</u> I come only as a beggar of God's mercy, unworthy, dependent on Him for everything. I certainly can't come as one demanding.

What If?

What if God never gives you anything in this life but Himself and His presence. You lose everything you hold dear because you choose Him, even your health and your loved ones? Will you still follow Him? Or do you want blessings in this life too?

God confronted me with this but at an even deeper level: if He never gave me the Spirit, would I stop following Jesus as my First Love? Like a man or woman who found the love of their life, yet the other person stalls. Do they continue to love, regardless, holding out in love and hope to their final day? Or do they settle for someone else? Which would show a First Love choice, permanently?

This was certainly a significant faith challenge for me.

Do I trust God even if He doesn't allow me 'in' during my normal lifetime? Could I be on my deathbed, still hopeful, still loving Jesus because He is worthy?

My answer was 'God, it will be deep agony if that is what You decide, yet I will follow Jesus regardless. I have made my choice. He is my First Love and He is worthy to be praised. I will not stop trusting You, however long it takes'.

I can only echo the words of Peter in **John 6:68** *'Lord, to whom would we go? You have the words of eternal life. We believe and know that You are the Holy One of God'*. I believe in Jesus and love Him, regardless of what God makes of my life. He is Sovereign, and therefore He decides over my salvation, my life, my eternity. I am entirely at His mercy.

We believe Jesus is the true God. Once we decide to follow, we lay down everything and follow, no looking back. It must be permanent and all-in. God will test me, perhaps even to my earthly destruction. Why does God test some deeper than others? I don't know. He decides.

Back to the implications for our faith then:

Is it my rightful expectation, demand and claim to receive salvation the moment I believe?

As the hymn 'To God Be The Glory' goes *'the vilest offender who truly believes, that moment in Jesus His pardon receives'* – I believe I satisfy God with my actions and expect salvation in return! The church says pray a prayer, therefore God must – is this not just a more advanced form of works, but similar with expectations?

What if God waits five years after I already served Him faithfully? Or 10 or 20 years? What if God delays for most of my life? Will I give up and either say 'it just shows I was saved all along', or 'there is no salvation – I have done it all and still God won't respond'? Will I go off in a spiritual tantrum and say God isn't fair? Does this not test why I came?

God wants followers of Christ solely committed to His Son so that they will abandon all to Him in love. They realise they have nothing to give to Him except their all and expect nothing in return, but beg for His mercy and grace.

We don't gain the crown of life for what we do, even to believe, but only by His grace

Perhaps you have been serving faithfully but you have not received His Spirit yet. Keep asking in full faith (*'without faith it is impossible to please God, because anyone who comes to Him must believe that He exists and that He rewards those who earnestly seek Him'* **Heb 11:6**). Perhaps God is waiting so your adoption into His family will be so sweet that you will never look back. Perhaps the blow torch of the life after salvation will be white-hot, and only salvation that came with the deepest agony will prepare us for what lies ahead. Salvation must be so precious that no fire will destroy it in the crucible of the life to come.

We may think of the years of committed service to God and how much we achieved for Him. So many elderly professing Christians struggle with seeking the true Jesus. They invested so much of their lives in their old religion that they don't want to give up what they spent a lifetime building up. It will make their lives seem to have come to nothing.

Let us put our decision to follow Christ beyond return, regardless of eternal or earthly cost or benefit. Let Him decide what to do with our lives. He is always in control but now I gladly yield to His will. How and when is God's choice.

And Yet!

And yet, He promises! His love and promises are certain and secure. Live in joyful expectation. Regardless of how long it takes, our full surrender doesn't change. Salvation awaits those who choose Christ at the deep heart level, whose names are in the Book of Life. *'Salvation belongs to our God, who sits on the throne, and to the Lamb'* (**Rev 7:10**).

It may be a faith challenge for you if you have waited for a long time. Don't lean back in resignation; make doubly sure God is not waiting for you to change your ways! He is your First Love and He is worthy. Your decision is fixed. You decided to follow Christ, keep following, keep serving, keep loving, keep stepping out in full assurance. Live it out. March on in faith.

Our daily marching around the city of God changes our heart and builds our faith until we do the only thing that remains for us to do – shout in faith in God! And He who is glorified by our faith, will do for us as He promised.

11 On the Narrow Road

The Real Purpose

Finally, we get to talk about the narrow road to eternal life in heaven. After such a long run-up this chapter may almost seem like an afterthought, yet this is the pinnacle.

God wants every human being to be on the narrow road, racing towards eternal life with Him

---

God put us on this earth to find Christ, to journey with Him and to complete the work that He ordained for us.

We may have lived religiously but without the Spirit, for many years. Our thoughts and lives will still be tainted by much of our old self. We may already have shed much of the earthly life outside the gate and this continues on the narrow road as our holiness grows under the Spirit daily.

Jesus leads and we follow. He is the Gate (***John 10:9***); now He is the Way (***John 14:6***), the direction, the purpose and the manner of the true life that follows. He is indeed the Truth, the Life, the Shepherd, the Bread, the Light, the Vine.

Heirs

Once we receive rebirth from God, it is almost unthinkable that we will be careless with this treasure. We've received the greatest prize in human life.

Are we now confirmed 'safe' for heaven? Is this what the Scripture teaches?

Yes!

... And No.

(We will get to this a little later)

By the Spirit we received God's seal and guarantee and we are experiencing a deposit of what is to come. *'And in Him, having heard and believed the word of truth—the Gospel of your salvation—you were sealed with the promised Holy Spirit, who is the pledge of our inheritance until the redemption of those who are God's possession, to the praise of His glory'* (**Eph 1:14**). In **Galatians 3:29** Paul says we are *'heirs according to the promise'*. **1 Peter 1:3-5** says *'He has given us new birth into a living hope through the resurrection of Jesus Christ from the dead, and into an inheritance that is imperishable, undefiled, and unfading, reserved in heaven for you, who through faith are shielded by God's power for the salvation that is ready to be revealed in the last time.'* There are many more similar references. What do they mean? That final salvation is certain and guaranteed for those who remain in Christ to the end.

God's promise and commitment are certain

We can be confident that God fights for those He calls His own. All heaven awaits the great wedding banquet. The Father already calls us children and Jesus already calls us friends, brothers and sisters in anticipation of the heavenly union. He wants us to live in certainty and in joy. We don't have to guess if we are His; we have the 'engagement ring' of the Spirit as proof. This certainty isn't possible for those who assume they are saved; they can only claim by positive confession.

This Is True Faith

John 3:16 shows its truth on the narrow road – *'For God so loved the world'* – now we know that love. *'Whoever believes in Him ... <u>will have</u> eternal life'*. Keep believing and keep having the claim on the inheritance. **<u>Romans 8</u>** comes to life with references to the Spirit that now apply to us:

- There is now no condemnation
- For those who <u>are</u> (already and remain) in Christ
- We have been set free from the spirit of sin and death
- We live according to the Spirit
- We are not in the flesh, but in the Spirit
- We are led by the Spirit because we are children of God
- We call the Father 'Abba' - <u>our</u> Father
- We suffer with Christ to be heirs with Him
- We have every hope
- All things work together for our good because we love Him and have been called to His purpose
- If God is with us, who can be against us?
- Nothing can separate us from the love of Christ
- We are more than conquerors through Jesus Christ.

For the first time these words are not mantras of a religion that we try to make our own by positive confession. For the first time the grace-promises are ours by birth right.

Only now do we possess the faith that pleases God (*'without faith it is impossible to please God'* **<u>Heb 11:6</u>**) and the definition of faith (**<u>Heb 11:1</u>**) makes sense – because we met the object of true faith – Jesus Christ. 'Believe in Jesus' is no longer a shortcut to a lie but the short form reference to the truth. This is the faith that lived in the faith giants of old (***Heb 11***). We step out to do what He says because He is our Lord, not because it is our reasonable duty.

Trials

'The just shall live by faith' (***Heb 10:38***)! We will experience many trials *'so that the authenticity of your faith - more precious than gold, which perishes even though refined by fire – may result in praise, glory, and honour at the revelation of Jesus Christ'* (***1 Pet 1:7***). Authentic faith brings glory to God. The faith of the Many does the opposite.

The lives of the Many will cause the nations to blaspheme God, because they do not see authentic faith and consider God a sham!

Do trials become fewer on the narrow road? My experience is they become more! Why? Because God is shaping us into who He wants us to be. He disciplines us out of love, so that *'it produces a harvest of righteousness and peace for those who have been trained by it'* (***Heb 12:10-11***).

God unties His children from this earth. He does not bind us to it even more by adding to our old worldly desires for comforts, fame and riches (so much for the Prosperity Gospel!) He brings fiery trials so that what is not of Him, burns away under its heat. Everything, even our most difficult trials, works together for the eternal good of those who love Him.

Perhaps God brings an issue that requires much faith and you step out in trust. Then He destroys the very thing you thought He would do or use to achieve a good outcome. But

God is still the One you can trust. He is teaching us not to look at the dense fog of circumstances, but to set our eyes on the Living God who allows or orders the fog and can remove it in an instant. He will do it in ways that will bring Him glory. He may delay the outcome in order to showcase His glory, like when Jesus delayed going to the home of Lazarus (**_John 11:1-44_**). Martha said Lazarus wouldn't have died if Jesus hadn't delayed. Yet God had something more spectacular in mind. Lazarus' family first went through agony as they lost all earthly hope. Then Jesus did a miracle that brought God great glory and as a single event probably had the greatest impact on strengthening the faith of the family and of other believers.

God parts us from our old ways and teaches us His new ways through trials

---

God gets great pleasure from our faith. He may prolong the journey while we wait for His promises in faith. The longer He waits, the greater the glory He receives! We want to end the agony and achieve the outcome quickly. We want to 'get on with life' yet God wants the closeness that comes from petitioning Him and drawing near due to the fire. He wants us to place our faith in Him rather than in people or things, especially when all evidence is to the contrary.

It brings God joy that we trust Him rather than trust Him for an outcome, especially if our journey is long and hard.

Fruit

John 15 speaks of the fruit God produces when we remain attached to the Vine of Christ. '_If you remain in Me and I in you, you will bear much fruit; apart from Me you can do nothing_' (**_John 15:5_**) and '_If you keep My commands, you_ *will remain in My love, just as I have kept My Father's commands and remain in His love* (**John 15:10**).

The Father prunes those who bear fruit, so our faith produces more fruit. Others are affected by the Spirit's fruit in us, often even without our knowledge. Not all fruit are spectacular but they are of eternal value and quality. There is more fruit because the excess of our lives is trimmed away and we become focussed on living for Jesus. The narrowing on Jesus and His work continues. Our talents are put to work and they produce a return under God's hand. We think we know our own talents, but only God really does because many of our talents aren't natural ones but opportunities and faith talents and for His glory.

Beware of a life of dedication of my own efforts and using my own talents – we do what we desire to do and dedicate the work to God, yet it more reflects my independent spirit. A life of surrender is the opposite: it is no longer we who live, but Christ who lives in and through us (**Gal 2:20**). We should have no preference how He uses us in His kingdom but wait on Him to guide me. Only this life bears eternal fruit. Work done without the guiding of the Spirit will burn away.

Whether God chooses to raise us up or cast us down, our task is only to please our Master. Since no true fruit comes from our own efforts, there is nothing for us to be proud about.

Guard Your Soul!

The narrow road is full of joy but it can be challenging and we can get discouraged. **Hebrews 12:1** speaks of running the race with a great cloud of witnesses (our great faith examples) surrounding us. We must do three things: 1) throw off what hinders us, 2) and sin that so easily ensnares us, and 3) run the race marked out for us to the end.

Throw Off What Hinders

What 'hinders' are not sinful things but what distract us, slow us down and risk the good works God saved us for. They may be good in moderation or as a one-off, but they can soon eat into our time with God and His service. Perhaps old things creep back into our lives or new things develop. It can cause us to become lukewarm because our focus is diluted or is elsewhere: Time spent in entertainment (TV, social media, socialising), work, sport, socialising, hobbies that become too important, even a 'good life' focus or plain laziness. Guard against old or new confidences and desires. Beware of useless, godless patterns that find their way back into your life.

The narrow road becomes more confined and more congested. Expect to trim down your life and to have God trim it. In the face of new Godly priorities our earthly life should lose its lustre. The old life, the selfish ways we spent time and money on trivia, self-seeking and the world, must end.

We are now a part of the Royal Household. Many old activities and behaviours are unbecoming of our new status and will pull us away from our true duty. This is not only vital for our own spiritual lives, but also for our example of life-stewardship to brothers and sisters and to unbelievers. Expect resistance, animosity and divergence even from the religious Many. Yet, let separation be as it may, our feet must tread firmly on the new narrow road!

It must remain my priority to search for Jesus in solitude, in Scripture, in prayer and with other believers. Even demands such as parenthood, care for others, or a busy work-life, must remain distant second priorities in our lives (it does not mean we neglect those things, but that they don't rule above God).

Our choices reflect our priorities and what we value most! We removed distractions while we were seeking Jesus; let's not allow them back in. If you become aware that you stray, repent and return! Put things beyond reach. Give God every priority.

Sin

We must guard against sin that so easily ensnares us. Ongoing wilful sin is incompatible with a Spirit-filled believer (*'No one who lives in Him keeps on sinning. No one who continues to sin has either seen Him or known Him'* **1 John 3:6**). We know the unredeemed by their sinful patterns, not only gross sins, but also unbroken anger, jealousy, gossip, etc. Our intentional obedience is required, to the end (*'We know that we have come to know Him if we keep His commands'* **1 John 2:3**). We won't live sinless lives, but by God's grace we will overcome! Yet we must fight daily with all energy and intent. Listen for His still, small voice. God's nature in us will show our sinful patterns and sin will become the greatest heartache for the saint.

Sin is like the smallest amount of diseased blood coming into our system, a virus so tiny that it is hardly visible under a microscope. Yet it can be deadly. There are no superficial cuts to the soul. Sin is also like weeds: they start as a tiny seed, they don't need tending, they grow by themselves. Pull them up when they are small. It takes the watchful eye of a Spirit-led mind to spot them early and a diligent and ruthless hand to destroy them quickly. You are the devil's target. To derail one true believer has greater value for him than keeping many enslaved - the harm to the name of God is much greater.

It is important that we judge sin on a Biblical rather than a cultural basis. Culture changes, God doesn't

---

What culture didn't accept 20 years ago may now be perfectly acceptable and even promoted. Culture may also accept many things that are unacceptable to God (*'What is highly valued among men is detestable in God's sight'* **Luke 16:15**). On the other hand, culture may not accept things that God mandates. <u>Let us only distinguish on the basis of God's expressed will and judgement.</u> His values and statutes are unchanging, eternal and we will be judged by them.

Stay Focused

Be confidently on God's side. *Be an **Ephesians 5** believer.* Read verses 1-20. The theme is in ***verse 15***: *'Be very careful how you live.'* It is so important to live the narrow road life, consistently, and to guard our souls.

2 Tim 1:14 *'Guard the good deposit that was entrusted to you - guard it with the help of the Spirit.'*

1 John 2:20 *'But you have an anointing from the Holy One, and all of you know the truth.'* This is not an anointing that we claim; it is given to us by our God Himself. Guard it.

The narrow road is congested so let us keep our faith alive and burning hot for Christ. Our souls need constant checking and filling (topped up) with the Spirit. Spiritual discipline has never been so important. Seek God's presence daily in solitude and prayer. Remain anchored in Scripture. Be resolute in obeying God in everything. Always keep your eyes fixed on Jesus who is the Author and Perfecter of your faith (**Heb 12:2**). Paul says *'I urge [beg] you, therefore, to reaffirm your love for Him'* (**2 Cor 2:8**). Directly translated this says 'keep on affirming your *agape* love for Jesus'. It is a lifelong task.

Hold earthly matters lightly: material things, desires, habits, even pain. Keep short accounts with God. Be faithful and diligent. Pray for wisdom (**Jam 1:5**). Let all be well with your soul (**3 John 1:2**).

God's Pleasure and Answered Prayer

When God answered our prayers before our rebirth we thought it was the proof of our correct standing before Him. In reality it was God's mercy to show us He exists and He is Almighty. He was drawing us to Himself and gave us every reason to believe Him and to have confidence in Him.

Now when we pray, God takes us on a journey, but this time as His beloved child. He takes pleasure in teaching us that everything He does is for our eternal good. For this He may take us to where we can barely hang on at times. He stretches our faith and clears out preconceived ideas. He may withhold or delay things we ask for. As in **Job 1:21**, whether He gives or takes away should matter less to us. Naturally it will impact on our earthly lives and it is bound to be hard at times.

Let us come to God in prayer, not looking to persuade Him, but to be persuaded of His will

---

Let us keep our eyes fixed on Him. Let us watch in amazement as He works His perfect will, and let us not defend or insist on our own preferred outcome. Since I died to myself, it is Jesus who lives through me.

God Guards Our Life in Christ... BUT!

When God brings us into His family, He promises to take care of us and that nothing will separate us from Him. God will never leave nor forsake us (**Heb 13:5**). We can stand on that promise with every confidence. The question of our closeness to Jesus does not depend on God, but on us ('Remain in Me, and I will remain in you' **John 15:4** NLT).

Luke 15 records three parables: The Lost Sheep, The Lost Coin, and The Lost (Prodigal) Son. Much has been written about the exact meaning of these parables. The context of the parables was the lost sheep of Israel who were part of the flock but were lost at that time.

But how do the parables relate to us as Gentile believers? Many interpret this in the context of evangelism – the Father going after the lost. I can personally not see how this can be about the unsaved being brought to salvation. Why?

Firstly, because each parable talks about those who belonged already. The Lost Sheep was already one of the flock. The parable doesn't say there were 99 sheep and the owner went to find one more to make a flock of 100. Jesus' words were '*Suppose one of you has a hundred sheep and loses one of them ...*' (***Luke 15:4***). You can't lose what you don't already have. The similar parable in ***Matthew 18:12-14*** is even clearer because both at the start and the end of the parable Jesus refers to '*these little ones*', i.e. those already of the faith. Verse 12 says the shepherd went after '*the one that wandered off*'. A sheep could not wander off if it wasn't a part of the flock.

In the case of the Lost Coin all ten coins already belonged to the woman ('*suppose a woman has ten silver coins and loses one*' ***Luke 15:8***).

The Lost Son was already one of two sons of the father and one left (***Luke 15:32***).

In each case, when the owner found the lost, they ask others to rejoice with them ('*Rejoice with me; I have found my lost sheep*' [***Luke 15:6***] and '*Rejoice with me; I have found my lost coin*' [***Luke 15:9***]). In effect it means 'I have found what already belonged to me but went missing'. The Lost Son decided he would say to his father '*I am no longer worthy to be called your son; make me like one of your hired servants*'

(**Luke 15:19**). A son means saved; a servant is in the house temporarily but a son is a part of the household (**John 8:35**). He says '*I am no longer worthy to be called your son*'. He was a son (i.e. reborn) but caused a great harm to the relationship. Also He was '*alive again*' (v24), i.e. was saved before.

Secondly, if this was about salvation and God was going after all the lost and found all, the parable will have to mean that God finds <u>all</u> people and brings them into His fold. This is universalism (i.e. everyone gets saved) which is un-Biblical.

These parables are therefore not about unbelievers being reborn, but about straying true believers repenting and being restored back into fellowship with God.

Why is this important? Because we must understand the distinction between believers who stray and God searches after them to bring them back, and those He doesn't.

The Lost Sheep and Coin

Through the Parables of the Lost Sheep and the Lost Coin Jesus tells of His care for those who fall away 'unintentionally' after their rebirth, and how He will come to find them again.

- The Lost Sheep tells how someone may become lost like a sheep not taking care and 'grazes itself into lostness'. God pursues and lovingly brings them home.

- The Lost Coin says if we lose our way due to a life event (the coin fell, i.e. perhaps a great loss, an unplanned life event that caused us to struggle and lose our way) He comes to get us. He will not leave us.

Romans 8:38-39 applies here '*For I am convinced that neither death nor life, neither angels nor principalities, neither the present nor the future, nor any powers, neither height nor depth, nor anything else in all creation, will be able to separate us from the love of God that is in Christ Jesus our*

Lord'. If we want to remain in Jesus, even if we lose our way temporarily, then God promises to come and get us. Nothing will separate us from His love.

Note: I know of people who came to true salvation under the message of the Lost Sheep. This discussion is not to cast doubt that they have were saved under this passage, but rather that I cannot see that it is its primary meaning.

<u>The Lost Son</u>

This brings us to where God does not promise to get us: The Lost Son (**_Luke 15:11-32_**). When we go after worldly and sinful pursuits wilfully, God does not keep us bound to Him.

It seems almost unthinkable that someone who encountered Jesus personally could consider this! God will warn us repeatedly to turn around, yet if we insist on going after the pleasures of this world (sinful relationships, etc.) and refuse to repent, then with the greatest sorrow, God will not force us to stay and does not pursue us.

What was the wealth the son squandered? God's grace. He spent his grace inheritance until nothing was left.

The son's condition was very serious and sorrowful. It contrasts with the Sheep and the Coin who Jesus said were 'lost'. Yet of the son Jesus said *'For this son of mine was <u>dead</u>*' (and is <u>alive again</u>); *'he was <u>lost</u>'* (and is found)' (**_Luke 15:24_**), which he repeats in **_Luke 15:32_**. If he did not turn back, his condition was terminal.

After all the love, care and provision he received at home, he was now worse off than the slaves at home. The son was starving even amongst the pigs (the epitome of uncleanness in Jesus' time) before he came to his senses. He had to realise his predicament and return in repentance and humility.

Some interpret the parable that, as soon as the son turned, God was there at his side, running to meet him. That is not what the parable says. The son was in a <u>distant country</u>. The father ran to meet him when he saw his son while he was still far off. He did not run to him in the distant country, but only when he was visible on the horizon. It was a long journey back.

God may allow us to return through much hardship to ensure we do not make light of leaving again, and the journey back may be a deep struggle. Not out of spite, but because He is jealous of His Son and His glory and protective of us. He is our Loving Father. When He sees we are truly on our way back for good, He runs to meet us and welcomes us with open arms.

We reap what we sow (of the same kind, good or bad), more than we sow (it always grows into more), later than we sow. If we return to sin and disobedience once we are on the narrow road, we will experience greater bondage and the wry fruits of our actions. Let us deal with sin quickly because the smallest pin prick may fester and accumulate. Do not imagine that, just because we do not see the immediate effect of sin back in our lives, it has not made a very deep cut.

'Remain in Me'

Receiving the Spirit is a great gift and privilege. That is why neglecting our relationship is a grave thing for God. It is to grow lukewarm and Jesus said to the Church in Laodicea *'So, because you are lukewarm—neither hot nor cold—I am about to spit you out of My mouth (**Rev 3:16**)*. This doesn't mean we'll be saved but just not on speaking terms with God!

God showed us His utmost mercy and undeserved favour when we met the Risen Christ. It is shameful if we don't then value our love relationship with Him above all else.

The Parable of the Ten Virgins (**Mat 25:1-13**) carries a clear warning: The ten virgins represent the future Bride of

Christ, waiting for the Groom, to be united with Him at the wedding feast. The lamp is the Word and the oil is the Spirit. All of the virgins have the Spirit as rebirthed believers. The five wise virgins ensured their oil lasted until the Groom came; the foolish ones did not. While the foolish were away to get more, the Groom came. The foolish returned to find the doors to the wedding venue shut and call '*Lord, Lord, open the door for us!*' but the Groom won't let them in. Yet, note His words '*But he replied, "Truly I tell you, I don't know you"*' (**_Mat 25:12_**).

It is interesting that in both **_Matthew 7_** and **_Matthew 25_** people call Jesus '*Lord, Lord*', however it is spoken by two very different groups of people. Of the **_Matthew 7:23_** group Jesus said He <u>never knew</u> them (no '*ginóskó*' – no personal, intimate knowledge), unsaved, un-rebirthed and therefore lost. Of the foolish virgins He says He doesn't '*eidó*' them. He doesn't 'recognise' or 'appreciate' them. They used to belong to Him but Jesus no longer recognises them as one of His own.

Let us place this in a lovers' setting. Jesus died for His love for all people. Then He gave the gift of salvation by the Spirit to the future bride. But some neglected the love relationship.

Now it's time for the wedding. The ones who neglected their love suddenly turn up for the wedding. They're interested again because there is a heavenly prize. But the Groom is deeply hurt. He says, 'I don't appreciate what you did' and 'I don't recognise you as My bride anymore. I gave you My all, but you neglected Me and went off with other lovers. Go away!'

Had the foolish ones returned and repented before it was too late, He would have welcomed them back ('*Here I am! I stand at the door and knock. If anyone hears My voice and opens the door, I will come in and eat with that person, and they with Me*' **_Rev 3:20_**). However, if they neglect this great gift and sacrifice (**_Heb 2:3_**) and don't return, their lot is sealed. We must take every precaution to guard the gift of salvation and the Spirit God blessed us with (**_2 Tim 1:14_**, **_1 Tim 6:20_**).

'Remain in Me and I will remain in you' (**_John 15:4_**). The first part of this sentence is our responsibility – 'remain in Me'. The second part is His promise 'and I will remain in you'. The first must be present before the second applies. He promises nothing will ever snatch us from His hand, provided we remain in Him.

'Once Saved, Always Saved'

Many argue that once we are saved, this salvation can never be lost again. I do want to touch on this. Where did we get this? From a full reading Scripture?

In contrast to the six popular 'proof texts' for claiming 'Once Saved' Always Saved', there are 10 times as many passages warning of falling away after we have been reborn. Almost all of the texts are in the New Testament with 10 passages directly from the mouth of Jesus Himself.

How can we disregard this mass of texts that speak the opposite way because we prefer the easy-listening promises?

I can but wonder: if we were alone on an island, with only the Word and under the instruction of the Spirit, could we ever have come up with 'Once Saved, Always Saved'? Would we ever have chosen a select few passages, yet denied the conditions that are spelled out in such abundance in the same Bible we get our assurance from? Why embrace the one, yet dispute with such vigour what appears 10 times more in the same Bible? It's just illogical!

God foreknew the humans He made. He knows we can be tempted to ignore His truth and His clear will. And it is almost as if He added 10 times more opposite passages so that we could never claim innocence. The warnings are everywhere!

Yes, God promises that nothing will ever pluck us from His hand, **if** we want to continue with Him. No circumstance, power, person or even Satan can remove us from Jesus if we want to stay with Him. And He will make every effort to keep us with Him. Yet, let us stick with His promises <u>and</u> take heed of the warnings that accompany His promise.

We must never take God's grace for granted (spending our inheritance). Let us not make up our own theology when God is so clear.

True believers shouldn't ask 'can I lose my salvation?' but rather say: 'With God's grace I will never leave'

<u>Falling Away</u>

If we fall away, i.e. not just temporary backsliding but renouncing the blood of Christ, we become useless to God and man, and are lost forever. It is then impossible to be brought back to repentance.

We won't spend much time here except to refer to two warnings that deserve our attention:

Hebrews 6:4-6 *'It is impossible for those who have once been enlightened, who have tasted the heavenly gift, who have shared in the Holy Spirit, who have tasted the goodness of the word of God and the powers of the coming age and <u>who have fallen away</u>, to be brought back to repentance.'*

Hebrews 10:29 *'How much more severely do you think someone deserves to be punished who has trampled the Son of God underfoot, who has treated as an unholy thing the blood of the covenant that sanctified them, and <u>who has insulted the Spirit of grace</u>?'*

But Who Is Asking?

Although this section is under the chapter about the 'saved' on the narrow road, it is worthwhile to note: It appears that the majority who argue salvation cannot be lost, may well be the ones who argue for salvation after a sincere prayer. <u>The salvation they defend so hard does not even apply to them</u>!

Having said that, I would never go so far as to say that all those who believe salvation is permanent are themselves lost. I am certain there are genuinely held views by saved individuals (and I have heard many such arguments from even well-known evangelical preachers), just as there are many who received the Spirit and consider this a second blessing.

For the vast majority of the proponents of Once Saved Always Saved I would say it seems if you are minded to disregard large portions of Biblical evidence on one crucial area to justify a deficient faith, this naturally spills over into keeping that false salvation. This should actually not come as a surprise. We either hold God's Word in the highest regard and want to find His truth, or we take liberties.

Follow on the Narrow Road

There remains so much to say about life on the narrow road and about living in the joy of knowing Christ personally, filled, guided and guarded by the Spirit. About enjoying the promise of being with God into all eternity soon. About marvelling at the love of the Father and His promises and provision. About seeing the miracles of God.

We could cover the life of persecution that every true believer should expect. We could stress the importance of continued obedience, diligence and guarding this most precious gift of salvation. Or how Satan will do everything in

His power to derail us and to isolate us. Yet at this point it will detract from the message of this book.

'Therefore, my dear friends, as you have always obeyed ... continue to work out your salvation with fear and trembling, for it is God who works in you to will and to act in order to fulfil His good purpose' (**_Phil 2:12-13_**).

'For this reason I kneel before the Father, from whom every family in heaven and on earth derives its name. I pray that out of His glorious riches He may strengthen you with power through His Spirit in your inner being, so that Christ may dwell in your hearts through faith. And I pray that you, being rooted and established in love, may have power, together with all the Lord's holy people, <u>to grasp how wide and long and high and deep is the love of Christ, and to know this love that surpasses knowledge—that you may be filled to the measure of all the fullness of God</u>' (**_Eph 3:14-19_**).

May we indeed grasp that love of Christ and be filled to overflowing with God's fulness! As soldiers for Christ we fight a glorious battle. To live in the presence of God and to head into heaven with Him is the prize worth having at any cost.

Let us take every step of the way seriously. Our lamps must burn brightly when the Groom comes.

12 A Major Divide, A Heart-Breaking Reality

This chapter brings together various points to highlight an important issue that is core to the church and for individual believers. We must consider this urgently and prayerfully before God for His clarity. They affect every believer directly.

Minor and Major Theological Differences

In the Christian faith there will be minor points of theological difference and these should never be divisive. Whether we interpret one way or another may be of theological interest or reflect how we express our faith but it does not change the fabric of faith in Christ or the sovereignty or essence of God or of Scripture. Scripture is clear the Body of Christ must be in unity, even in the presence of minor differences.

Then there are major points of difference on core truths, central to true unity. It is not for individuals or churches to agree to disagree but to establish what God says.

A Major Point of Difference

What can be more important for the church than to know when someone is saved in God's eyes? The church exists to glorify the name of Jesus and to build His church - the community of saints, so how can we fulfil the Great Commission if we do not have God's light on what salvation is?

Many in the church may want to argue for silent Spirit rebirths when we give our lives to Jesus, yet for all the reasons we discussed, this is just not true. According to Scripture the Spirit enters each person individually and incontrovertibly at rebirth. These two positions are irreconcilable. Ignoring this would account for the salvation of the Few and the damnation of the Many ('*I never knew you*').

This leaves us with a major dilemma and a major point of theological difference, at the core of the earthly church. How can we claim to be 'church' if we do not possess the definite Spirit? Any 'practical agreement' amongst Christians, whether verbalised or implied, that does not agree with the fullness of Scripture, is not just a different opinion. It is false!

Churches and whole denominations appear to subscribe to the concept that the Spirit was given to the church in Acts, and we share in the Spirit by our self-certified faith in Christ. Therefore, most would subscribe to a non-essential but useful 'Second Blessing' to a select few followers at receipt of the true Spirit. (There is of course also a major disagreement around what constitutes the true Spirit rather than the demonic.)

The assumption that rebirth takes place at our decision renders God passive in giving salvation and relegates Him to decide over a 'second blessing' only (exclude 'strange fire' here). God's basis for giving the Spirit is also unclear.

Is this an issue? YES. It is a major issue.

When we count the small number of genuine Spirit rebirths amongst Christians we soon realise why Jesus said 'Only a Few' will find life. The church has its own 'practical understanding of salvation' that it perpetuates.

We widen the tent unilaterally, without God. We may add many converts to Christianity and a false salvation, yet Jesus is Saviour and Lord to only the Few in the inner sanctum.

Implications

Understanding true rebirth and the baptism of the Spirit as a single event has considerable implications for the church:

1. Those who think they are saved without the definite Spirit, remain lost, even the church calls them saved and after many years of dedicated service.
2. If the church continues to assume salvation, people are damned in their millions, unknowingly.
3. The church counts amongst its 'saved' members vast numbers of unsaved.
4. Only those who subsequently receive the 'blessing' of the True Spirit, are in fact saved. But they weren't saved before, regardless of their past sincere faith confession.
5. The lack of Spirit baptisms would also account for the powerless ministry we see world-wide as many (most?) ministers of the faith are not actually saved themselves.
6. The true church, the Bride of Christ, is only a fraction of the active church. They are dotted across the world, with greater concentrations in some areas and churches.
7. It explains the church's lack of respect for God's Word.
8. It accounts for the manner in which the institution of the church goes astray – they never met the true Christ!
9. Without the power and truth of the Spirit, Christian values erode at an alarming rate. The divide between the world and the church becomes wafer thin. The church predictably capitulates to worldly lifestyles and cultural values. This stands in sharp contrast to the true church, holy and set apart.
10. God's name is being blasphemed due to the sham of worldly Christianity.

11. Our vast pastoral load results from pastoring an unrepented, unsaved membership. Members perpetuate the lifestyles and vices of the unsaved. It also accounts for growing social issues in our churches such as divorce and ungodly lifestyle choices.

12. The falling away of the church in the end times will be massive. Those who are superficially attached will have few qualms about taking 'pragmatic decisions' for their own earthly benefit when the fires of the end times come.

13. The greatest sadness is that if followers knew they were not saved, would many not have searched further? We deprive them of the opportunity! The church is culpable!

The Greatest Burning Issue

A Biblical understanding of salvation is so important and the church must grapple with it seriously before God. Besides recanting on the existence of the One True God and salvation through faith alone in Jesus Christ alone, I cannot think of a greater issue for the church to wrestle with today. We must know when someone is saved in the eyes of God!

Understanding salvation is core to the church's existence

Professing Christians will choose whatever is most palatable for their earthly comfort. Sadly, for the Many, the awakening will be a minute too late, when there's no more opportunity to change.

Oswald Chambers said: *'One life totally devoted to God is of more value to Him than one hundred lives which have been simply awakened by His Spirit.'* We can be awakened to who Jesus is and even to our own sinfulness. Yet, if we are not reborn of the Spirit, we will remain a clanging cymbal.

Churches, leaders and church members, what will we do? Will we continue to build our houses on sand to our own destruction, or will we turn to the rock of God's truth?

If it costs a lifetime of ministry, a seat at the top table or the ridicule of the earthly church, will we remain proud and protect our earthly ministries, positions and relationships? Or will we humble ourselves before God Almighty? We have a grave responsibility before God!

A Heart-Breaking Reality

The Truth and the Worldly Church

The Truth

The central greatest issue for mankind is the Truth. There is One Central Absolute Truth: Jesus Christ. **John 18:37-38** records the following exchange between Jesus and Pontius Pilate *"For this reason I was born and have come into the world, to testify to the truth. Everyone who belongs to the truth listens to My voice." "What is truth?" Pilate asked'*. Jesus came specifically to testify to the truth! If we miss what He said, or if we choose only a part of what He said, we miss the truth of God Himself.

The Bible is God's written Truth; everything in His Word is His facts. If we believe or proclaim something different or try to soften God's facts we and/or others are in serious jeopardy because His facts don't change. His Words are certain and what He says, IS. It is ridiculous to we think we can change anything by our interpretation. Instead our only hope is to find His meaning and live by it. What can we gain from projecting our human wisdom (foolishness) into it?

The Church and the Truth

The purpose of the church is to live out and preach the truth of Christ. The church is not an organisation, but the body of true believers, each marked and indwelt with the Spirit. Yet, in the main, the modern church no longer is the Body of Christ, but a religious pursuit that associates with the name of Jesus and lives from preferred titbits of the Truth.

The Many in the church fail to understand that snippets of Truth don't make for the Truth, but a LIE. The moment we divorce God words from the entirety of His message and select passages, we end up with a man-made religion. Within this setting we now find the mainstream of churches associating with the Word but living in falsehood!

The message of many churches is falsified not so much in what it teaches, but in what it leaves out. The Many in leadership themselves don't accept the Truth of Christ which He came to testify to. They don't believe it, haven't been reborn and therefore don't teach it.

It is truly heart-breaking that the very church we trust to teach the truth, does not do so. Many people trust the church for guidance but are being led astray by the church itself! Thankfully there are exceptions! Yet we cannot have confidence that the typical church will lead us in the Truth of Christ, regardless of its number of years in existence, its size or however well-respected its leaders are.

Who Is To Blame?

We may want to blame leaders for the situation and that may in part be true. They are the ones with theological study, it's their profession and they should be the ones leading us.

And yet we are the church. We read the Word of God, we don't take it seriously, we live and believe as we will. We want our ears tickled. What Paul wrote to Timothy 2,000 years ago applies equally to us: *'For the time will come when people will not put up with sound doctrine. Instead, to suit their own desires, they will gather around them a great number of teachers to say what their itching ears want to hear. They will turn their ears away from the truth and turn aside to myths'* (**_2 Tim 4:3-4_**). Paul was not just talking about the wayward but of every religious believer who refuses to give up and won't repent. Instead we agree our own definition of sin, God, Jesus, salvation and the Bible.

Furthermore we choose leaders who will perpetuate what our 'itching ears want to hear'. Yet, while there is a collective 'we', of much greater importance is 'I'. I am responsible before God. I perpetuate falsehood when I don't take God and His Word seriously. Predictably we then end up with a false Gospel within the church when I am a part of that church!

Some Tests to Apply

Test yourself and your church by the following Biblical truths:

Do you understand, and does your church teach:

- if we love anything else in this life more than Jesus, we cannot be saved? That it isn't a question of saying the words or loving superficially, but that God tests whether it is true at the core of our being?

- if we don't give up all that we are and have, pick up our cross daily and die to ourselves, we cannot be saved?

- that to follow Jesus means to leave behind the old life, that following Him costs our entire lives in the natural, otherwise I cannot follow Him?

- that without Godly sorrow and true repentance there is no salvation? That continued sin is evidence of lostness?

- that salvation isn't just a matter of only believing in Jesus but that the evidence of the truth of my professed faith and love for Christ lies in submitting to Him at the heart level in everything He commanded, and that without this evidence, there isn't salvation?
- that salvation is on the basis of the blood of Jesus alone by God's grace alone and that I don't deserve salvation because I claim to believe?
- that only the definite Spirit rebirth is salvation and shows His approval and authentication of that faith?

If you do not believe and proclaim these central truths of Scripture, then your faith is built on false hope. There is still time to find true salvation in Jesus Christ. Take it seriously!

If your church does not speak these truths clearly and consistently, then it is preaching a different Gospel and you should seriously question whether you should be there. There is real danger in staying in a half-truth: being surrounded by easy teaching rather than the truth of Christ it will affect our own walk; it never leaves us the same. Think carefully whether that is the right place for you, even if it costs you all the closeness that you thrive on amongst 'good Christians', soothing messages and energetic singing. This is not what the church is about! We are there for one reason – to find and worship the Almighty God in Jesus. True fellowship comes after Truth.

Please do not let the opportunity go by to become a son or daughter of the Almighty God. It is worth giving up your entire life for.

13 Parting Comments

We've reached the end of a marathon journey!

Life's only true success is when we become a child of God through faith in Jesus. Everything else is temporary and pales into insignificance. What does it help to gain every material thing, every love and every accolade in this life and live to 120 years, yet regret it into all eternity? Only Jesus makes life worthwhile, and all else are the trinkets of a lost life.

First Love

Perhaps now you have studied the evidence you will agree:

The core problem of the church is how few have met Jesus personally and been reborn of the Spirit

---

They never started the race. DNS!

Many professing believers unknowingly 'play for the other team' because they were guided the wrong way and never checked the truth in the Bible for themselves. They won't know their error until they get serious, or it will be too late.

There is lots of space in our churches for the idea of Jesus: His salvation, His love and His grace and mercy. There is plenty of space for a Jesus who will make us into something: better servants, powerful ministers, adorable leaders, greater musicians, helps us in our time of need and gives us peace and joy and a good life. Yet there is hardly space for a ***Galatians***

2:20 Christ: *'I have been crucified with Christ; it is no longer I who live, but Christ lives in me'* and for the Jesus who demands a First Love relationship, evidenced by obedience.

In the majority of our churches there is no or little space for the real Jesus of Scripture, but only one of its own making.

<u>More importantly, though, there is NO space before God for what the vast majority in Christianity call 'church'.</u> How desperately sad that the True God and the church are almost mutually exclusive! Jesus said *'when the Son of Man comes, will He find faith on the earth?'* (**Luke 18:8**). His expectation is there will be preciously little.

Satan has the secular world and its religions under His influence. Unfortunately he also has the vast majority in the Christian church under his influence.

God does not accept every effort and every sincere faith. Faith that does not satisfy God is worthless for salvation

---

Our faith can never be untied from the First Commandment: *'Love the Lord your God with all your heart, with all your soul, with all your mind and with all your strength'* (**Mark 12:30**). It remains our yardstick.

Centrality of the Bible

The Bible is the Word of God. It is our responsibility to find the truth that God communicates. He says *'... I am God, and there is no other ... I have made the end known from the beginning ... My purpose will stand, and I will do all that I please ... What I have said, that I will bring about; what I have planned, that I will do'* (**Is 46: 9-11**). Do you believe that? How does this affect the way you read Scripture?

Choose Life!

There are two versions of Christianity, of God, of Jesus, of the Spirit, of salvation and of the truth. One version is true, the other is false. The true version brings the greatest triumph; the false version leads to the greatest catastrophe. The true is true only within the narrowest confines of one small Gate and a narrow Way. The false becomes wider by the day.

God said to Israel *'This day I call the heavens and the earth as witnesses against you that I have set before you LIFE and death, blessings and curses. Now choose LIFE, so that you and your children may live and that you may love the Lord your God, listen to His voice, and hold fast to Him. For the Lord is your LIFE ...'* (**Deut 30:19-20a**). Take a moment to read the whole of Deuteronomy 30. Note the repeated emphasis on obedience, love for God and the promise of LIFE.

God says today: Choose LIFE!

The essence of the decision we make for Jesus is that we hand over this one life we have on the earth, for Him to live through me. This one life with our loved ones, our job aspirations, our homes, cars, financial independence and securities, our physical appearances and vanity, intellect, lusts, hobbies, pets, everything that we are about and that defines us, even our Christianity. This one life we value so much, whether expressed in fame, fortune, dreams of a good life, earthly loves and pleasures or in hate, anger, unforgiveness, jealousy, envy and unbelief. But in reality we are not giving up, but trading up, because we receive vastly more in return.

Many years ago, when God systematically dismantled my earthly life of jobs, positions and security, I once cried out to Him in desperation: *'I just want my life back'*. And very quickly the reply came as clear as day: *'Choosing Jesus means you leave behind the life you once had, forever.'* Afterwards someone gave me the very apt word from Scripture: *'No one who puts a hand to the plough and looks back is fit for service in the kingdom of God'* (**Luke 9:62**). I knew it was me!

That old life is over, forever. By God's mercy and grace I now have a new life with a new Master and with new priorities.

We cannot waver between two lives. We cannot have the earthly life and add Jesus to it. The choice is clear: it's one or the other

---

What If?

What if everyone spoke well of you as an amazing Christian and even a leader – can you admit you are lost?

What if the True Christ's message takes you away from what your church teaches? Or contradicts what a much-loved one taught you? Can you accept God's discernment that even the sincerest Christian example you respect may never actually have found Jesus themselves? Even well-known speakers, authors and evangelists that you admire?

What if following Jesus in His way brings division in your life, even in your household? What if it costs the life that you know?

What if you dedicated your life so far to what you thought was the truth, worked in ministry or charity, fulltime or not, and now found the right path?

Are you prepared to lose face and change direction for Jesus, even if it costs a lifetime's ministry, or your standing in the church? Or will your reputation in the earthly church weigh more (*'many of the leaders believed in Him; but because of the Pharisees they did not confess Him, for fear that they would be put out of the synagogue'* **John 12:42**)?

Will you lose everything you worked for and lived all of you life, for the sake of the truth of Christ? Even after a career in ministry or in charity and in doing good? Can you cast away as worthless a lifetime of a dedicated work for Jesus and call it with Paul 'rubbish' for the sake of knowing Christ and Him crucified, even at this late stage in your life?

A Message to Leaders and Evangelists

A single passage in Scripture that should tell us the wider church is terribly deceived about salvation is **Matthew 10:37-38** *'Anyone who loves their father or mother more than Me is not worthy of Me; anyone who loves their son or daughter more than Me is not worthy of Me. Whoever does not take up their cross and follow Me is not worthy of Me.'* We cannot read that passage and think most people in our churches are saved, because the most basic check on priorities will confirm it simply isn't true! Surely this passage condemns most of an average Western church, if not most leaders too!

What a terrible predicament!

Leaders, Teachers and Evangelists: ensure you know Christ, confirmed by the True Spirit! After that you have a glorious opportunity to speak the truth of Christ consistently and clearly. Don't be concerned about the size of the Bride of Christ - God looks after that. Our responsibility is to lovingly proclaim the full Gospel, help people find the small gate and encourage them onwards on the narrow road. I encourage you with my deepest and most fervent prayers to be diligent in Christ with the true Gospel, even if some (or many) will leave because they want their ears tickled.

Final Words

Please continue to investigate the contents of this message in the Word of God for yourself. Read every reference, in context. Pray, ask God for His wisdom and revelation. My faith and certainty are of little use to others.

The following short poem by Geoffrey O'Hara verbalises God's revealed heart in a warning to professing believers. We would do well to stop and meditate on this:

> *Why call Me Lord, Lord and do not the things I say?*
> *You call Me the Way and walk Me not!*
> *You call Me the Life and live Me not!*
> *You call Me Master and obey Me not!*
> *You call Me Bread and eat Me not!*
> *You call Me Truth and believe Me not!*
> *You call Me Lord and serve Me not!*
> *If I condemn you blame Me not.*

If you realise you are not reborn yet, then I pray for your Paul's prayer for the Ephesians '*And I pray that you, being rooted and established in love, may have power, together with all the Lord's holy people, to grasp how wide and long and high and deep is the love of Christ, and to know this love that surpasses knowledge – that you may be filled to the measure of all the fullness of God*' **Eph 3:17-19**).

May God bless you with His wisdom, His discernment and His salvation in Jesus Christ! Amen.

It has been my privilege to share this message with you. Thank you. If you wish to contact me, please email me on

daniel.j7x7@gmail.com.